WHAT
SHOULD
ABOUT YO

THE CLIO MONTESSORI SERIES
VOLUME 4

WHAT YOU SHOULD KNOW ABOUT YOUR CHILD

Based on Lectures Delivered by
Maria Montessori

CLIO PRESS
OXFORD, ENGLAND

© Copyright 1989 by Clio Press Ltd.

Reprinted 1995

This edition has been licensed for publication by the Association Montessori Internationale, Amsterdam. *What You Should Know About Your Child* was first published in 1961.

British Library Cataloguing in Publication Data
Montessori, Maria, *1870-1952*
   What you should know about your child.—(The Clio
   Montessori series; v.4).
   1. Children. Personality. Development. Theories of Montessori,
   Maria, 1870-1952
   I. Title
   155.4'18

ISBN 1-85109-096-7

ABC-Clio Ltd.,
Old Clarendon Ironworks,
35a Great Clarendon Street,
OXFORD, OX2 6AT, ENGLAND

Typeset by Megaron, Cardiff
Printed and Bound in Great Britain by
Hartnolls Limited, Bodmin, Cornwall

Cover design by CGS Studios, Cheltenham

CONTENTS

PREFACE

I am very proud that my work and my sentiment for children have awakened in a lofty personality such as Mr. Gnana Prakasam so much interest as to induce him to spend valuable time and so much intellectual concentration upon the production of this book.

Refined interpreter that he is, he has been able to bestow the light of simplicity to ideas difficult to understand. In this book, which promises to be of great aid to the diffusion and understanding of my work, the reader will not merely find lessons exposing ideas and my interpretation of the soul of the child, he will read through the clarity of vision of a psychologist who has contributed his generous efforts to link my thoughts to the mind of the public.

My gratitude goes as homage to Mr. Gnana Prakasam who has come forth to protect the interests of the child and has stretched his hand to help him to ascend.

MARIA MONTESSORI
Adyar, 5th February 1948

FOREWORD

Dr. Montessori in her above Preface says I have interpreted her. This is true, particularly as regards the essential truths underlying her Method of educating children. I have spared no trouble in distilling the essence from her books and lectures as well as from her career and work. Her approval is a reward. But that approval, though a valuable imprimatur of authenticity, is not my whole aim.

Has Dr. Montessori got at the basic truths underlying the child's nature, growth, development and functions? Is her Method conducive to the shaping of the most efficient, service-able and happy men and women of the future? In answering these questions the reader may take into account the world-wide expansion of the Montessori System. But each individual reader must give the verdict after ascertaining whether, according to his or her knowledge, observation and conscience, the relevant facts stated in this book are demonstrably true or not.

Such realism as implied in the above paragraph, such independence, such self-reliance, such discipline in activity and service, such happiness in achievement – these are the essentials of the Montessori System as the following chapters will indicate and as the character of the schools and the pupils will prove. The reader has to see whether Dr. Montessori interprets Nature correctly and follows Nature's laws. Truth and reality are the tests. This way lies Scientific Education.

A. G. PRAKASAM
Law Library, Colombo, 1st May, 1948

DR. MONTESSORI

A BIOGRAPHICAL NOTE BY

THE EDITOR

Dr. Montessori was born in 1870. Having decided on a medical career and having mastered the natural sciences, she obtained at the University of Rome an M.D. at the age of 26 years, distinguishing herself by securing a double honours degree as Doctor of Medicine and Doctor of Surgery. This was in 1896, Dr. Montessori being the first woman in Italy, and probably one of the few women in Europe at that time to become a Doctor in the Faculty of Medicine. This was sound scientific equipment for future achievements.

From 1896 to 1911, for nearly 15 years, Dr. Montessori practised medicine and held the Professorial Chair for Hygiene and Anthropology. In 1898, in the course of her professional contact with children, she became interested in education and in 1907 she opened the first institution for children below 6 years which was called House of Children and which became her Educational Laboratory. A period of intense study of childhood and marvellous practical results followed.

In 1909, her historical volume, called in English *The Montessori Method,* was published and was translated and read in most of the countries of the world. 1913 was a memorable year as it was then that she gave her first International Course of Lectures and visited the United States. In 1916 appeared another epoch-making book by Dr. Montessori called by its English publishers *The Advanced Montessori Method.*

In 1919 she visited England inaugurating an International Training Course in London. Her work spread into every country in Europe, was taken up by the Dominions and was welcomed in India and South America. As a consequence the Association Montessori Internationale (A.M.I.) was founded in 1929 at

BIOGRAPHICAL NOTE

Elsinore with the aim which was stated as follows: "Spreading knowledge of how the child, immature and struggling to discover and develop his own powers, may be assisted in his task of self-realisation and of reaching his full perfection of growth."

In offering to Dr. Montessori the Honorary Fellowship of the Educational Institute of Scotland at an enthusiastic meeting at Edinburgh in 1946, the President said: "Teaching is a conservative profession, but once in a generation there arises an outstanding figure which comes with a breath of new life inspiring people to new endeavours and to new activities. These are the great figures of Educational History. Among them no one in our generation stands higher than Madame Montessori. Her name has become a household word, not only in Scotland, not only in Europe, but in every part of the world."

The above is a tribute to Dr. Montessori by an Educational leader in a country like Scotland which is always in the vanguard of educational progress.

Dr. Montessori, in principle and practice, offers a strong hope for mankind to build the peace and progress of the world on the strongest foundation, namely a free and democratic education of the children of the World.

WHAT YOU
SHOULD KNOW
ABOUT YOUR CHILD

1

SCIENTIFIC EDUCATION

The Montessori Method is scientific education. Knowledge of childhood is its foundation. It is built on the discovered laws of the development of the body and mind of the child.

The march of science in modern times has been incredibly rapid. The human mind has unravelled myriads of secrets of the exterior world. The series of inventions and discoveries have been astonishing. The nature and the laws governing the physical environment of man are minutely known. Equal attention and care are now being given to the study of the Human Mind, the Human Intelligence and the Human Personality which are responsible for all achievements.

The scientific endeavour which is the characteristic of our age, the systematic examination of facts and ascertainment of principles and acting upon them, these procedures which have been successfully applied to discover the material world, must also be persistently directed to aid Human Life. Life includes Mind, Intelligence and Personality.

Thus education is an aid to life. It is the protection of life. It is a help to life according to its own laws of development. Success in education clearly depends on understanding the secrets of life with a view to serve it the better, with a view to develop the great energies within man in strict normality.

If education is an aid to life, two conclusions are inevitable. The first conclusion is that education must begin with the beginning of life itself. The second conclusion is that education must assume an aspect very different from the one it has assumed for ages: education can no longer retain the form of mere *teaching* with which it has been synonymous up to the present day.

WHAT YOU SHOULD KNOW ABOUT YOUR CHILD

If education is a help to life and if education begins with life itself, what education can we give to a new-born baby? What help can we give to a child of six months or of one year? An answer will be: We can help the child by nursing, feeding or giving hygienic care. Evidently the person who gives this answer forgets that the child from the beginning of life has a mind as well as a body, that the child has both a mental and a physical life. If education is a help to life, it must help development both in the physical field and the psychic field.

This brings us to the problem: What is the nature, what are the conditions, what are the needs of the psychic life of the child in its early stages? Are there any natural or ascertainable stages or periods of mental development? What are their characteristics? What sort of help or education can be given at these stages or periods? It is the answer to these questions with which the Montessori Method is first concerned. This inquiry is called Child Psychology or the Science of Childhood on which the Montessori Method is based. Ours is the study of the Psychology of the Child from its very birth and from its very beginning. "It is not true," says Dr. Montessori, "that I invented what is called the Montessori Method. I have studied the child, I have taken what the child has given me and expressed it, and that is what is called the Montessori Method."

4

2

HELPING THE CHILD TO

HELP HIMSELF

Pre-primary Montessori Schools are called Houses of Children. Our idea of a school is not a building with four walls in which to enclose and confine children but a house wherein children are their own masters. This idea implies the necessity to prepare for the children a world of their own, where their minds and bodies can find suitable activities. The teacher should be a guest in the House of Children, or someone who intends to help them, or someone to be of service to them.

One of the first ideas that was born together with the beginning of Dr. Montessori's educational work was the idea of giving to the children specially suitable furniture of their own. To say this today is to say nothing new; but at the time when this idea was put into practice, it was startling. That was forty-three years ago.

At about that time Professor Dewey made a valuable discovery. He was a professor in the University of Columbia in New York City. He made up his mind to make a tour of the shops in that wonderful city for the purpose of buying, not toys for children, but articles which might be suitable for use by children. For example, he looked for furniture, tables, chairs, cupboards and benches for children. Wherever he went the shop-assistant said: "No sir, nothing of that kind is available." He then tried to obtain towels, dishes, dinner-sets and basins suitable for children. But he met with no success. Then he wrote his opinion in a sentence which has become famous. That sentence contained the following thought: "The world, as far as the external environment is concerned, has forgotten the child."

That statement was true. But Dr. Montessori had undertaken the work of education for children. She said "If houses suitable for children do not exist, then let us build them. If articles suitable for children are not being made, let us get them made." What things to make and how to make them had to be found out by experiment and experience. Thus, not only pieces of furniture but so many other things suitable for the children were made to order.

Thoughts are institutions. Often from a simple idea great consequences arise. The outcome of the above idea was not merely that the children served themselves by using these objects, but the ultimate result was that the children changed their character by using these objects. They showed a creative joy in using them. The joy was different from the normal joy of children at play.

Thus there was opened up a new way, a new method. The special needs of the growing bodies and minds of children were kept in mind. Here was the vision of a method for a solution to the problem of the freedom of the child, and also for the solution to the problem of the occupation and conduct of the child. We shall now proceed to give details of these problems.

Mothers often say: "My child is exasperating," "He has fits of temper," "My child wants me to be with him always," "I cannot get away from him a moment" and "My child is easily bored." Other mothers say "My child is boring," or "He always wants stories and the whys and wherefores of things." Now these are problems arising out of occupation or want of suitable occupations.

There are also problems of conduct. Some parents say: "My child is bad. How am I to make the child good?" or "What are we to do with the child? He is mischievous. Are we to beat him or not to beat him?" In this and many other ways the child presents many problems both in the family and in the school.

There is a further and fundamental problem, the problem of the freedom of the child. The distinction between Democracy and Totalitarianism has still to be faced. Is the child to be left free to form himself or is he to be formed? The question of the freedom of the child and the freedom of nations demands an urgent solution.

Nowadays most people believe that it is necessary to give freedom to the child. So the family faces the problem of how to leave the child free. Giving freedom to the child is not one problem. It involves problems upon problems without an easy solution.

That is why it was a happy moment when the House of Children came into existence. It pointed to a solution. There was a failure on the part of the adult to understand the needs of the growing mind and body of the child and a failure to provide for those activities which are needed for his development. The House of Children was a solution.

Let us see what happens in a family where the adult rules. Let us go back forty-three years when the science of childhood or the laws of child development were ignored. Then, as now, mothers loved their children and took great care of them; bathed them and washed them, dried and powdered them, clothed and brushed and combed them, and took them for a walk, and attended to all their physical needs.

But let us consider the mother, whose child climbs upon an arm chair or sofa, and who says in a threatening voice to the child "Get down at once," or the mother who under similar circumstances says gently "Now dear, get off from there please." Each of the above mothers has her own way of correcting the child.

Yes, as you can well imagine, it is a matter of indifference to the child whether the mother uses angry tones or endearing ones, since the main object of both mothers is the same; both the angry mother and the affectionate mother are preventing the child from doing what he is doing. If the child wanted to sit on the steps of the staircase he is told at once: "Oh! don't sit in that dirty place." Whether the prohibition is sweet or bitter, prohibition is a prohibition.

If you follow this matter of stopping a child from doing things which, according to adult ideas, he should not do, you will find that the child is in the same position as the poor people in the great city of London, for example, who attempt to sleep somewhere. They first try the churches, only to be driven away from there by the voice of authority which says: "Get out." They then try a park bench, but they are unceremoniously pushed out. Ultimately, they are obliged to walk about the streets the whole night, not being allowed to sleep anywhere.

So it was with the child. He was not allowed to use anything which surrounded him in the adult environment. "Hands off" was the standing order given to him as regards many frail or valuable things which were in the possession of adults and intended for their use, like a porcelain cup, a watch, an inkstand or other precious breakables. The child was allowed to touch practically nothing in the adult environment.

He was given a rubber ball or a toy and told to play with it. But he soon threw it away. Not knowing that the child also may have some reason for complaint, the parents had a complaint against the child and said: "As soon as I give a toy to my child he breaks it or throws it away." The sad aspect of this behaviour of adults is the tyranny, which the child feels, of being stopped in every attempt on his part to be active: he is being thwarted in his natural yearning for physical and mental activity; he undergoes the torment of being repressed at every turn.

The mother or the nurse may be unconscious of her tendency to repress the child continually. But the fact is there. The child's yearning to use its eyes, ears, hands, legs and limbs, its striving to master the details of its environment, to apply its mind to the surrounding objects and to gather knowledge directly from things—of these matters the mother or the nurse is unaware or ignorant.

Another serious matter is the superfluous help which is given to the child. Such help is an actual hindrance. Every good mother assists the child to dress, combs its hair, takes it for a walk and does many other things for the child. Some mothers say: "It is our duty to do everything we can for our child. The more we do for the child, the better mothers we are." We wish to point out that beyond a certain point every help given to a child is an obstacle to its development.

There was a mother who was much admired by everyone. This mother used to say that until her children were twelve years old she always bathed them herself. People said "What a wonderful mother!" In those days it was not realized that it was not enough to merely supply the physical needs of the child; that the most important need was the need of helping the child to help himself. It was not then realized that the child needs to be independent, that such aids and props were not conducive to giving the child that independence which is necessary for its growth and development.

Giants patronizing and helping pygmies will end in a short time by reducing the pygmies to utter incapacity and helplessness. The kindness of the giants will become the bane of the pygmies. We must give children service that assists development and not service that obstructs development.

3

ACTIVITY AND

INDEPENDENCE

Under the urge of nature and according to the laws of development, though not understood by the adult, the child is obliged to be serious about two fundamental things.

The first is the love of activity. It is coupled with the desire to accomplish things. These are worth while and important to the child. From the point of view of the adult there may be nothing serious in the child's activities or accomplishments. But the point of view of the adult is irrelevant to the fulfilment of the child's vital and necessary functions. A serious part of the child's activities is to imitate the adult. The child accomplishes this in his own way. He does not reason about it. But this imitation is important in the formation of the social man of the future.

The second fundamental thing is independence. All the efforts of growth are efforts to acquire independence. A matter of vital importance to an individual is that he should be able to function by himself. In order to grow and to develop, the child needs to acquire independence.

When does the child need to begin to do things by himself without our help? The answer is simple. The child needs to do things by himself from the beginning of life, from the moment he is capable of doing things. This urge is revealed again and again by the child. We have so often heard children of a few years of age say: "Help me to do it by myself." By helping the child to do things by himself you are helping the independence of the child.

This help can be given to the child by furnishing him with what we give in the House of Children. In the House of Children we give him objects which he can handle by himself and which he can learn to master. This principle can be applied, and must be applied, in the child's own home. From the earliest possible age the child must be provided with things which may help him to do things by himself.

It is by helping the child to help himself we render him that help which will make him independent. To teach the child to brush his hair, we must give him a small mirror, a small comb and a suitable brush. If we want the child to wash his hands we must provide him with things fit for his size. He will rejoice in his being able to do things. He will do what he does with enthusiasm. Thus the child is introduced into a form of life which is necessary for him.

The above will involve some problems. There is the problem of the mother who says "I can wash ten children in the time which one child takes to wash himself." This brings us to the necessity of having an institution in which children can engage themselves in these actions peacefully and without inconvenience to others. This points to the necessity of a House of Children where things are provided according to their needs; where occupations suitable to them are available; and where an understanding teacher is prepared to help them to do things to which they have a natural liking. Such a teacher will not, in the bad old way, obstruct children by doing for them what the children can do by themselves.

To an adult onlooker the activities in our Houses of Children may not appear to have any immediate utilitarian significance. But these activities are means of development. They satisfy the child's yearning to use its eyes, ears, hands, legs and limbs, to apply its mind to the surrounding objects and to gather knowledge directly from them.

Apart from the mastery of details and initiation into independence, the activities in the Houses of Children solve other problems. The very self-occupation and pursuit of objects to be achieved remove defects of thought and conduct. The scope for suitable activity obviates the possibility of repression, whether of the sweet variety or the severe variety. These points will be developed later.

For the present we wish to emphasize the need for providing for those activities for which the child has an almost insatiable appetite. The mental hunger of the child is as real as the physical hunger. We shall illustrate this mental hunger by means of physical hunger.

Suppose you are hungry and you had nothing to eat. A person comes to you and says, "You are unfortunate, I am so sorry for you. I will pray for you. I hope you will find someone who will give you something to eat." Another person to whom you appealed says, "Get away, Clear out." Neither the one person nor the other satisfies your hunger. It is a matter of practical indifference to you whether you get the pious treatment or the rude treatment. Neither treatment satisfies your hunger.

Just as a child who has physical hunger is irritable and intractable, so is a child who has mental hunger for activity, for development, for exercise of his mind and spirit. The solution for the physical hunger of the child is to feed the body. The solution for the mental hunger of the child is to feed the mind and spirit of the child. It must be added that if someone else eats the soup for you, you will not be strengthened.

We shall conclude by illustrating the necessity for independence. Let us take walking. The child has an urge to walk by himself and not to be carried about by others. After a certain time he succeeds in doing so. Is it not true that parents are filled with delight when the child begins to walk by himself? Who are the parents who wish to stop the child from walking by himself because by walking he may go away from the parents? Have you heard any parent say, "I do not want the child to walk by himself because I want him to be dependent upon me"?

On the other hand have you seen a fifteen year old child being carried in someone's arms? This may not be done physically but parents and teachers are doing the same thing mentally, morally and figuratively in several aspects belonging to the child. Such help is thoughtless unkindness. It is a hindrance. In short the whole problem of education is to give the child the necessary help, excluding any unnecessary help, so that the child may be helped to develop himself. This means that the adult must re-orientate himself in his understanding of the child and thus assist in the solution of a great problem. Self-activity thus becomes the basis of education.

4

NATURAL LAWS

OF DEVELOPMENT

The new approach to education must be based on natural laws of development. We have to avoid, in leading the child, the path of severity. We have also to avoid the path of repression even if it is coupled with sweetness. We have to follow the straight path of nature according to ascertained laws of development.

These natural laws of development apply to plants, animals and children in definite and unalterable ways. Now let us first take the child.

The child is a great builder, a great constructor. If you ask yourself: "Who has given me this power, this intelligence, this knowledge which I have?" you may answer, "It is a child that has made me into what I am." Your father could have died before you were born and you might have had the same power, intelligence and knowledge as you have now. Your mother could have died as soon as you were born and you might have the same power, knowledge and intelligence as you now have. But if the child who made you had died you could not be here.

This cannot be denied. This is the greatest fact of nature. The child is the constructor and maker of the adult man. The child is the father of the man.

We are not trying to overthrow the great sentiment and veneration which we owe to our parents. But we wish to secure for the child a sense of gratitude and affection similar to that which we bear towards our parents so that we may not consider the child as the product of the adult, but regard him as the producer of the adult. It is only a cycle in which both adults and children take their places and it is necessary to recognize the parts both play and the relative importance of each.

NATURAL LAWS OF DEVELOPMENT

You may say: "This is all very nice but what does the child do? He does nothing but grow. Who is making the child grow?"

There must be some divine force which enables the child to make himself. In this connection we may also ask: "What does the mother do?" She also waits for the time to pass, and when the time comes, the child is born. When the child is born, he is already a human being with eyes and ears and legs and limbs. But what has the mother done? She has merely waited and allowed the child to make himself.

Can the mother say: "I shaped the nose of my child in this fashion, or I gave this shade of colour to his eyes, or I moulded this limb in this manner?" She has only waited. The child evolved himself. The great dignity of the parents comes from the fact that they have made a vital contribution to the coming into existence and development of the child. But the miracle of life remains. The miracle occurs as much in the vegetable kingdom as in the animal kingdom or among children. Plants follow their own laws of development; so do animals; so does the child. But there is a parallel between the development of a child and the development of other living beings.

As an example let us consider the development of a chicken. In the hen's egg is a yellow substance which is called the yolk, besides what is called the white. In the centre of the egg is a very tiny white spot. It is upon this small spot that the creative force works. If we put this egg in an incubator and we leave it at the proper temperature, after closing the drawer, and wait for twenty-one days, then we can see what has happened. We open the drawer. It sounds as though someone is knocking. There is something knocking from within. All of a sudden the shell of the egg breaks. Out comes the little chick. It is covered with yellow down. It has brilliant little eyes, already able to see. Its little feet are already fit for the purpose of walking.

Most certainly this little baby chick was not made by the mother hen. Yet according to Nature's ways, the mother hen has a task to fulfil. Supposing there is no incubator, she undertakes her duty of hatching the eggs in earnest. A strange fever comes over her. A spirit of intense love for her eggs fills her and drives her to sit on the eggs in order to give them the necessary heat. It is the love of the mother which ensures that by her brooding over the eggs for three weeks they will have all that is necessary to enable them to hatch.

When the eggs are hatched the hen continues to care for her offspring. She gathers them under her wings, keeps them warm and protects them. She teaches them to peck on the ground. The chicks follow her example. They learn by doing. You can see how happy the chicks are around their mother. The mother hen has given the chicks her love, warmth and sacrifice; but she has not *made* the little chicks.

As another example let us take the development of the silkworm. In the beginning there are little spots like grains of sand, similar to the white spot in the middle of the hen's egg. After sometime, lo! out of these little grains emerge little worms. Now they have to be fed. This little worm is a vegetarian. It is strange that he feeds himself with the leaves of one particular tree and no other.

What a glutton the silkworm is! He eats and eats. He grows and grows. But what would have happened to the poor silkworm if he did not have these leaves to feed upon? In Nature it is so ordained that the eggs are left to hatch on this special tree.

What has happened to the butterfly which laid these silk-worm eggs? She died as soon as she had laid her eggs. She laid the eggs in a place where her little ones would be safe. She fixed the eggs on a tree whose leaves alone are the special food of her offspring; the butterfly never has a chance to see the silkworms who are her children. There is a mysterious law and command which the mother butterfly has to obey. She has, however, provided the silkworms with the conditions and facilities necessary to enable them to make themselves.

Utilizing the conditions provided for him, the silkworm starts his self-activity. He builds up the wonderful structure known as the cocoon. With one continuous thread he makes the chrysalis which has invariably the same form. Man utilizes the cocoon to make beautiful dresses for ladies, vestments for priests and robes for princes and many other garments in what is termed natural silk. The achievement of the silkworm was according to the laws of Nature.

It is possible to provide many examples in the vegetable or in the animal kingdom to show how organisms form themselves by self-activity. Let us end with the picture of the majestic oak which as it grows has no dependence whatsoever on its mother tree. This is creation's secret.

Growth and development through self-activity is Nature's greatest miracle.

The development of every organism has to be accomplished within the precise space of time allotted to it. We know to the exact minute how long one particular little germ will take to develop. There is no one more attached to the time-table nor so faithful to it than any little being in the process of growing. There is no finer example of perfect obedience to the laws of Nature than the phenomena of creation. It is a sort of obedience which does not admit the possibility of disobedience.

Is it possible, where everything obeys a mysterious command, where everything is subject to the fulfilment of a plan, that man alone should have no laws according to which he should develop? All we need to admit is that man creates himself according to the laws of growth and development. Men are often blind to this fact. This unconscious concealment prevents the miracle from revealing itself to us.

A leaf springing from a bud is an organism developing under your eyes; it is the same with flowers; an embryo undergoes progressive changes and every change is at a particular time, according to a particular schedule. A child who is born on earth without speech, without reason, without co-ordinated movement, becomes an independent being, who speaks, understands and moves. Is it possible that this comes about without obedience to commands or laws of Nature?

The laws of development are there. They have to be observed, ascertained and followed. The child should be given the freedom to develop within the laws of natural development.

5

PERIODS OF DEVELOPMENT

To study the laws governing the development of an organism it is necessary to study the characteristics of the periods of its development. Life is the principle of activity and adaptation which is seen in every organism. We shall have to refer to two aspects of life. The first aspect is physical life. The second aspect is mental or pyschic life.

Life is one unity. In the beginning there is one great adventure. That adventure is birth. From the very beginning of life after birth, from the first hour, certainly from the first day, there are traces of the existence of a psychic life. In other words there is evidence of the functioning of a mind.

The psychic life of the child does not come into existence all of a sudden. It follows that there must be some form of psychic life even before birth. It also follows that the psychic life of the prenatal period and the psychic life of the period immediately after birth must be different from the ordinary mental life as we know it. The chief characteristics of ordinary psychic life are purposeful activity and the power of reasoning. From birth the child passes through various periods of physical and mental development. We shall now proceed to examine these periods. There is a parallel between the physical and mental development of the child.

The first period of child development is the period from birth to the time when the milk teeth are replaced by another set of teeth. This period extends from birth to about six years. The second period ends with the attainment of puberty at about twelve years. The third period goes up to about eighteen years. It is at eighteen years of age that the wisdom teeth begin to appear. The wisdom teeth indicate that the physical organism is reaching maturity. After the age of eighteen the development of a person does not end. That age however fixes a boundary in the life of the child.

You may say these divisions are too arithmetical to be real divisions of life. But the physical landmarks and parallel mental qualities are clear at about the sixth, twelfth and eighteenth years of life. It must be remembered that there are no exact time limits applicable to all cases. The above periods represent averages. There are oscillations, backwards or forwards, from the average. The oscillations are individual differences.

There are some children who, at six years of age, have completely replaced all their milk teeth. There are others who get their second set of teeth a little later. Similar individual differences may be observed in the emergence of the wisdom teeth. The study of the facts relating to each individual is important but, as there are several thousand million individuals in the world, the stated average forms a useful working basis. The average is also a guide for the study of any individual case.

The time limits for the above periods are affected not only by individual differences but also by differences due to sex. There are appreciable differences between men and women in this matter. Thus the working averages already mentioned become all the more useful. The time limits of these periods were recognized from ancient time and acted upon.

But there is a difference. The old educators divided the life of the child at school in relation to the syllabus of instruction which was to be given to the child. The modern educator is more concerned with the natural characteristics and developmental requirements of the child than with any syllabus of instruction framed merely for the sake of tutoring the child in adult knowledge. But it is encouraging to think that both the ancients and the moderns are in agreement as regards the average time limits of the three natural periods of child development which we have stated.

Let us now consider the period from birth to three years. This period has hitherto not been taken into account by educationists because they took into account only that part of life in which it was possible to impart knowledge. As it was thought impossible to impart any knowledge before three years of age, this period was eliminated from school life. For the same reason, even a study of the nature, characteristics and needs of children of this age was neglected or ignored.

Up until a short time ago even children from four to six years were eliminated from education on the grounds that they were too young to be taught. It must be remembered that, in the old sense, teaching was identical with education.

When educationists did begin to consider some sort of education for children between four and six years of age they called it pre-primary education. This attitude presumed no real education could be given before about six years of age. We have already seen that the educative process should start as early as the birth of the child and the development of the child does not begin abruptly at any age.

The problem of education is how to provide suitable conditions and facilities for the development of the child at each stage. Education during the period from birth to three years has always been left to the family and has been entirely in the hands of parents or guardians. At present there is a tendency to educate children of about three to six in special schools which have been started in different countries. These are called Nursery Schools.

In our Houses of Children we admit children between two and a half and three years of age. They continue there until they are six years old. For this reason the principles and methods of education relating to children of this age will receive in this book special and detailed treatment.

But each life being one entity, every successive period is only a further development of something which has been established in the previous period. Although in these chapters attention will be focused on the needs and requirements of children between three and six years, the study of the preceding and subsequent periods of childhood cannot be ignored or excluded. Our educational work is gradually covering the whole educative period up to maturity and beyond.

In the pre-natal period the child has established all the vital organs which after birth are developed. In a parallel manner the foundations of psychic life have been established. Though there has been much development in the pre-natal period, the development of a child during the first three years after birth is unequalled in intensity and importance by any period that precedes or follows the rest of the child's life.

The next chapter will deal with the first three years of life.

6

THE FIRST THREE
YEARS OF LIFE

If we consider the transformations, adaptations, achievements and conquest of the environment during the first period of life from zero to three years, it is functionally a longer period than all the following periods put together from three years until death. For this reason, these three years may be considered to be as long as a whole life.

Because of the accelerated progress in all directions in this concentrated period of three years, when we receive a child of three years in our House of Children, we may say we are receiving a man who has lived for a very long time. In terms of arithmetic the individual is three years of age. In terms of vital development he is a man who has accomplished a whole cycle of life and has lived a whole life of experience.

It is not wrong to say that we are welcoming to our House of Children a hero who has made a great conquest, who has fought many battles and won them, who was wounded many times, suffered and recovered. He who comes to us may be regarded as a man venerable with age and acquisition, not a child of three. If you consider the matter carefully you will see there is something more than growth in the first three years of life. The child before us is something which borders on the marvellous.

Let us examine more closely the child of three years who comes to a House of Children. When he was born, so far as movement was concerned, he was a paralytic. Now he is able to walk and to run. At times he runs so fast that it is difficult for adults to catch him. This achievement is a comparatively minor one. There are much loftier phenomena.

The child is able to understand almost everything in the house, in the compound, on the road and in the neighbourhood.

WHAT YOU SHOULD KNOW ABOUT YOUR CHILD

If you scrutinize carefully you will understand the multitude of things around him which the child understands. You may mention the names of any person or thing and the child knows what you are talking about. The achievement of the child is almost unbelievable. This achievement was necessary for the child.

The child had to make a personal conquest in order to perceive and understand everything which is around him. His achievement is the result of observation, the fruit of personal study. In a short time he has been able to see many things, recognize many things which take a much longer time for the adult to do. What he has acquired was not given to him by Nature. It is the result of his own activity.

We often stress what a great adventure birth is. Think of yourself being transported to a new and completely different country from your own. Suppose for example you were left all of a sudden on the Moon. The change would not be as great for you as the change which affects the child when it is born into this world.

The child finds himself in a world which is new in every sensation and in every shape. An adult going to a new country has had some experience of another country. What experience has a child had of this world before he comes into it? Yet, in one year, two years, three years, the child is able to do what it may take an adult twenty years to do.

It cannot be said that the child is born with things necessary for his life, or that he came into this world with a quantity of knowledge. No matter where he is born he achieves the same miracle. If he is born in a small fishing village the child takes in all the things that are there with the same facility as that with which another child born in New York takes in the big buildings, the motor cars, the aeroplanes and the noise. It is a personal achievement.

This points to his possession of a power which adults do not possess. As an illustration let us consider the marvellous facility which children of this age have in mastering languages. You may say that this facility is natural, inborn, hereditary. This is not all. Sometimes credit is given to the mother for the learning of a language by the child. For this reason the language "taught" by the mother or learnt by the child at first is called mother tongue. Now, this opinion is not quite true.

THE FIRST THREE YEARS OF LIFE

It is not universally true that the mother "teaches" any particular language or languages to a child. The baby who has lost its mother at birth learns to speak a language just the same. The mother is not there.

Suppose an Italian mother brought her child to New York. After a while the child talks with an American accent. The mother had nothing to do with this performance. She does not know the American language or the accent. The child speaks it as fluently as any child in New York.

The fact is that it is the child who learns the language. He learns it well. He learns it better than any of us can, no matter how educated or painstaking we are. The most curious fact is that all children have this facility of learning languages within the same period of life all over the world.

Another strange thing is that the child imbibes any language with equal facility and zest, whether the language is easy or difficult, whether the language is primitive or advanced. If you go among certain African tribes whose languages are not yet fully developed and contain a small number of words, you will find the children absorbing the prevailing language or languages with the same readiness as that with which children master the current language in England or France or Germany or Italy where the language is very difficult and contains a large number of words.

It may be noted that children use a language as correctly as it is used in their environment. The facility in the learning of languages through sheer self-activity is an example of the facility with which children of this age make conquests of their surroundings in so many other respects.

It is clear that there are so many things, which according to the laws of development, the child can do with ease in this period and which he cannot do so well later on. The child has a method of approach which the adult cannot imitate. If the adult is going to help the child, the adult has to learn from the child. This understanding will help the adult to allow the child to develop according to the characteristics of each special period of development.

We may now summarize the position of a child coming to a House of Children at three years of age. During the first year after its birth the child has developed into a man who knows how to direct himself, how to recognize objects, how to think, how to talk and how to walk. In the second year the child builds himself up further and increases his mastery of the environment. During the third year, before the child comes to a House of Children, the child consolidates all the conquests he has made during the previous years. The House of Children thus takes charge of a person who has developed through his own efforts and achievements without any help except the creative impulse which enables him to make himself.

7

MORE FACTS ABOUT

CHILD DEVELOPMENT

There is at times a sudden physical growth in an organism. When this occurs the individual becomes delicate in health and easily falls ill. He is also mentally less alert than he was. In other words, physical development takes place at the expense of mental development. Approximately in the first two years of life there is an enormous development physically; yet the mental development is still greater.

Let us now look at the physical development. At the age of six months a child's weight is twice what it was at the time of birth. When he reaches the age of one year his weight is three times what it was at birth. When we state the facts in this manner you may not be impressed by the magnitude of development. That is why the use of imagination becomes necessary.

Suppose you had a friend who weighed 150 lbs. Suppose you met him again after six months and he weighed 300 lbs. Suppose that you met him once more at the end of a year and he weighed 450 lbs. In relative terms that is what happens to the child. You may imagine the magnitude of his development during twelve months.

When such physical development takes place in later life on a much reduced scale, mental powers seem to diminish. It is not so during the first few years of life. An enormous physical development is accompanied by a still greater mental development.

At about two years of age all the mental faculties are formed and functioning. The powers of perception, memory, imagination and reasoning are keen and remarkably active. The child is vigorously utilizing all the implements necessary for the conquest of his environment in every respect. Psychologists are realizing more and more the importance of the first few years in the life of the individual.

We shall now mention a few facts to show that the embryonic development started before birth is continued with intensity for a few years after birth. This is seen in the action of certain glands whose secretions flow into the blood and of whose flow there is no outward sign. One of these glands is that which determines the colour of our skin. There are others which have a direct influence on the absorption of calcium, which is the main substance in the construction of our bones. There are other glands which regulate the absorption of sugar when muscles are formed. These glands start their work in the embryonic period and continue their activity after birth also.

Similar to the above is the development of the cerebellum which is a part of the brain. The growth of the cerebellum helps to bring about a sense of equilibrium in the child. It is, therefore, after the beginning of this development of the cerebellum that the child begins to sit up. The later development of the cerebellum helps the child to be able to stand up and walk by himself.

During the first months of life the cerebellum is very little developed. Then at about six months after birth it starts to develop with rapidity and continues to grow until it reaches a considerable volume. This growth lasts from six months to eighteen months. Then it grows gradually and slowly until four and a half years.

From the above facts it is clear that many important things are happening to the child at about six months after birth. It is at six months that the first signs of hydrochloric acid are found in the child's stomach. It is also at about this time that the child's first tooth appears. The above two facts indicate that the child is now capable of digestion and needs other food than milk.

The importance of the teeth in the development of the child has to be emphasized. Nature makes use of the teeth as milestones in the development of the individual. Whenever there is a change in the teeth it is a sign that something important in the whole individual is taking place. It may be noticed that in the embryonic stage there is the design of what is going to take place afterwards, and teeth are among the earliest parts of the design.

MORE FACTS ABOUT CHILD DEVELOPMENT

We have already indicated the significance of the appearance of the first tooth at about six months; all the other milk teeth appear in about two and a half years after birth. We have also indicated the significance of the replacement of the milk teeth by another set of teeth at about six years and also of the emergence of the wisdom teeth at about eighteen years.

We shall now deal with the mental development of the child in these initial stages. This is concerned with the relation between the child and the environment. The child gathers impressions of the outer world by means of his senses. The organs he uses for this purpose are his eyes, ears, and hands as well as the organs of touch and smell. Language also has a sensorial aspect as it consists of sounds.

Mental development at this stage is a process of awakening. The child needs to be aroused by outside stimuli. Light and sound, smell and taste and touch, form and figure and landscape, appear to call and invite the child. We may say almost a social relation must exist between the child and his environment so as to produce the necessary development.

It is at the early age of one month that the child begins to need these calls and invitations from the outer world. If you take the child to a garden he looks at things very calmly without any excitement. Repetitions are needed to awaken his interest. To create a cycle of relationship, it is advisable to take the child regularly to the same garden or park for some days or weeks.

If you observe small children, you will see that they interest themselves in so many things in which you thought a child would not be interested. You will see how they absorb the environment, quietly at first, but very actively as months proceed.

There is an idea that a child must sleep the whole time. For this reason even when the child goes out he is taken in a baby carriage all covered up so that if there is anything to be seen he may not see it. But is the child born to sleep? We must give a chance for the urge for self-development in the child even at this stage. The child is born to see, to hear, to know, to enter into relationship with the outer world.

Some people may say: "These new ideas are all right. But were not children brought up well in the past without these methods?" The reply is that these new ideas are necessary on account of the new order of things. In the olden days children did not sleep all the time; they were not away from their mother, almost all the time; they were not taken care of by a nurse or any other substitute.

In the olden days the child went wherever the mother went. The food of the child was in the mother. Therefore the child was always near the mother. When the mother moved about in the home or the garden or the field, she always had the child with her. Nature had made provision for the child's entry into the relationship with the external world by placing the food of the child in the mother herself. New methods are now necessary because the old order of things has changed.

There are now practical difficulties in putting the child in touch with the external environment in the early stages. Under modern conditions new needs exist. Modern solutions are necessary for modern ills.

Similar to the necessity for contact with Nature is the child's need for social life. At six months of age the need for social life in the child is so great that if he be left without it, he falls ill and may even die. This may seem exaggerated but it is a proved fact. We give an example below.

In a city in Holland there was an institution which aimed to teach poor mothers how to bring up their children in a hygienic manner. There is no place in the world cleaner than Holland. The above institution was run very well. So careful was the doctor in charge that he studied children's individual differences in food and fed them accordingly. If there were scientific perfection in the treatment of children in relation to food and hygiene, such perfection was found in this institution.

The children were kept isolated from each other and were well protected against any accidental infection. Everything was measured and precise. The rooms, the beds, the dresses, and the nurses were spotlessly clean. But something was wanting. All of a sudden most of the children became ill. With all the hygienic care given to the children, the possibility of an epidemic was inconceivable.

The physicians in charge set about trying to discover the cause of the prevalent illness. They realized that something vital was missing. It was noticed that the children who came to the neighbouring dispensary with their mothers regularly for treatment did not contract this strange illness, though they had all the disadvantages of apparently non-hygienic living. Then as some of the children in the hygenic institution were at the point of death, it was thought advisable to allow the sick children to remain with their mothers in their own homes and to receive the natural attention, affection and simple treatment of which their mothers were capable. The children were quickly restored to health and the peculiar illness contracted in the hygienic institution disappeared. The mental and spiritual vitamins given to the children by the parents were superior to the physical vitamins given in the hygienic institution.

The need for social life, the need to go out and see people and converse with them, is a great part of the need of the child to have communion with the outer world.

8

LANGUAGE

Language is the most powerful instrument of human progress. The child masters language during the earliest periods. Observations have already been made about the facility with which the child in the first years of life conquers its linguistic environment. In view of the importance of language in the development of the child, this chapter will be devoted exclusively to this subject.

What is language? It is merely a number of sounds. Sounds uttered by the human voice have not in themselves even the attractiveness of a bell when it is rung. They have no meaning except the meaning which men have given to them. Yet when the sounds are joined together into words and uttered in their current meaning, they convey from one person to another ideas and emotions and every aspect of reality and experience. By means of language the experience and knowledge of one individual are transferred to another individual; the experience and knowledge of one generation are transferred to the succeeding generation; and in the form of written volumes, languages contain the accumulated knowledge and experience of mankind in relation to every art and science.

Having been used and developed by generations of people for centuries, a language reaches a high degree of perfection as a vehicle of human thought and expression.

We have already referred to the astonishing performance of the child in acquiring during the first few years of life the language of his environment. It is noteworthy that one of the earliest acquisitions of the child is language which will be of the utmost assistance to the child in his future progress and advancement.

We shall now mention a few scientific facts about language and its use by the child. Those who have studied the subject have noticed a great disproportion between the capacity of the child to understand a language and his capacity to express himself in spoken words. This means that the number of words which a child understands is greater than the number of words which he uses to express himself. This is a general fact about the human mind. Most of us have stored in our minds more thoughts than we are capable of expressing and more words than we can use.

When this phenomenon was occupying the attention of scientists, certain discoveries were made in the organic field. It was discovered that there are two centres in the brain concerned with language. One is the receptive centre in the brain which records spoken words; and the other is the motor centre which is in operation when we talk. The existence of the two separate centres was put forward as an explanation for the disproportion between the quantity of words recorded by the receptive centre and those sent out from the motor centre.

The following may illustrate the disproportion. In a sales store there may be an enormous number of articles for sale, but only a few of these articles may come into contact with the members of the public who come to buy them. Something similar happens with the words stored up in the mind. In speaking we are capable of using only a portion of the words recorded by the receptive centre. A mystery yet remains; because we know only those words or thoughts that come out of an individual. As regards other thoughts or words, we can only make deductions.

Here is another fact relating to the development of language. The development of language in a child is not gradual or uniform. There is a small acquisition and then a pause; and suddenly there appear big acquisitions. We cannot say there is irregularity in the development; but there is an absence of gradualness.

At about six months after birth, you wake up one morning and you hear the child making noises, pronouncing syllables always the same, like ma, ma, ma, ma. In order to arrive at syllables like those above there has been a long preparation which began almost at birth itself. At the age of one year there comes the first real word spoken by the child. By the first word we mean the first word which the child uses to designate a person or object.

Between the sixth month when the child utters the first syllable and the twelfth month when he pronounces the first real word, there is a great amount of attention, observation, imitation and very hard work, ending with the first linguistic victory in the form of the first articulate word. After a further six months, another important thing happens.

At about the eighteenth month the child begins to use substantives or the names of things like table, dog, or bread. The child seems to have discovered that everything about him has a name and takes special interest in the things around him, particularly in their names.

Three months after the child uses a few substantives as described above, he begins to use a large number of words. We may say there is a real explosion of words. During the explosion all kinds of words are used, nouns, verbs, prepositions, adjectives or adverbs.

Within a few months after this explosion of words there is a similar explosion of sentences. The child begins to use all kinds of sentences. He has learnt to join one word to another to form a sentence and is able to make sentences to express almost every variety of thought. This crescendo of linguistic victories brings the child to about two and a half years of age.

The above are the chief stages in the learning of language by the child. There are other remarkable phenomena to which we now wish to refer.

The first significant syllable uttered by the child at about the sixth month was preceded by a process of listening. Besides this aspect which affects the ears, there is the process of taking impressions of speech through the eyes.

You may notice that a child of four months observes with intense attention the mouth of a person who speaks to him. How does this attention to the sounds of human speech arise? Can we say that the child used its reasoning power to watch the mouth of the person speaking to him? Did the child anticipate and execute a logical plan of watching lips and listening to words before he was able to babble the first syllabus conveying meaning?

There is clearly a mysterious urge making the child go through these processes in their rational sequences and focussing his special attention, spontaneously, on the mastery of the sounds which make up the language of his environment.

It cannot be said that the child is a mere living machine which records sounds and reproduces them. If so the child ought to register all the sounds which the environment presents to him and be able to reproduce them. For instance, the children of a village hear every day the words of the people who speak around them as well as the sounds of the cows and buffaloes in the village. Yet when the children begin to make the first sounds, they do not reproduce the sounds of the cow or of the buffalo.

In the big cities of America and Europe trains come into and go out of stations almost every minute; and there is almost continuous whistling. Usually there are many slums close by, where poor people are crowded together so that their children hear constantly the whistling of the train. Yet there is not a single case of a child who, when beginning to express himself, does so by whistling.

Though the child hears them, he does not reproduce the simple sounds of the cow, the buffalo, or the train; yet he is capable of distinguishing and reproducing complex sounds which run, one into the other, as those of language. The child is capable of the tremendous efforts involved in mastering a language in such a short period of time.

If we went to China, even if we did not know the Chinese language, we should know that there is some language being spoken and that the sounds which the Chinese were uttering had some meaning. This is not the case with the child. When he comes into the world he cannot be said to realize that there is a thing like language. It seems clear that there is a mysterious urge towards the self-activity involved in the acquisition of language by the child. There grows in him a gradual consciousness of an urgent need which he supplies with his own efforts.

During the first years of life, particularly during the first two and a half years, the child has an extraordinary capacity to master language, which adults do not possess. We wish to refer to a few remarkable aspects of this capacity. Without any aid from adults, or any instructions in grammar or syntax, the normal child speaks the home language grammatically and obeys the rules of syntax. Even prefixes and suffixes which are mere particles to give slight modification to the meaning of words are appropriately used.

There are certain languages which contain minute differences of sound to show whether a noun is masculine or feminine or whether it is plural or singular. The child knows these differences and incorporates them in his speech. This is not all. In order to make sense, the words in a sentence must be arranged in a certain order. In some languages the verb is placed at the end of a sentence; in other languages the verb is put in the middle. In some languages the adjective precedes the noun it qualifies; in others it comes after the noun it qualifies. The child has mastered all these details without the assistance of a teacher or grammar.

The achievement of the child is not a mechanical happening. It is something greater. It is the performance of a human intelligence which, placed among the stark realities and requirements of life, forges for itself the mechanism of expression and a vehicle of communication with the outside world. In about two and a half years the child has mastered a language which for the purpose of receiving ideas from others or expressing his own ideas is as satisfactory a medium as perhaps a foreign language learned by an adult after twenty years of laborious study. As the child grows this medium develops in intensity and extension. But for practical purposes it may be said that at four and a half years of age a child's linguistic conquest of the environment is almost complete.

There is a peculiarity in the language which the child has mastered as his original medium of expression and communication. This language is suffused with a sentiment and affection in relation to the early environment of the child and forms part and parcel of his personality. It has been pointed out that the original language which is sometimes called the mother tongue and which has been mastered by the child by his own spontaneous activity without the unpleasant associations of books, teachers or lessons, is the best medium of the child's self-expression and of artistic compositions.

What would happen if the child did not learn the language merely by living, merely by his own efforts, and if he had to have a teacher to teach him to speak his original language? Imagine how many schools of language and how many thousands of teachers would be necessary to make the children of the world speak their own language. And how many people would remain dumb and speechless for life for want of sufficient schools or teachers to make the children speak their own language.

LANGUAGE

But fortunately for mankind the child is endowed with a marvellous power, which adults do not possess, of being able to grasp the language, to absorb it from the environment and to make it a satisfactory medium for expressing his ideas and receiving ideas from others within the first few years of his life.

The child is thus a collaborator of the very first importance in the formation of civilization. We may say that the child is the very basis of civilization. It would be almost useless for man to possess intelligence if he had not the power of expression which the child acquires by his own efforts.

The child is endowed with a mental power which is different from ours. It may be said that the child is able to conquer language because he is in a creative state and the adult has passed that state. The child's method of receiving impressions from the outside world appears to be a method quite different from ours. This mystery may be explained by the following comparison. What is given below is a figure of speech and should not be regarded as a description of what really happens.

The child's mind appears to be like the sensitive plate of a camera. Supposing we wish to take a photograph of a landscape, what do we do? We expose before the landscape a sensitive film. If in front of this film there be one person or hundreds of persons, the film takes the impression with the same indifference. Whether the people in front of the sensitive plate are all dressed in the same way or differently, the film registers whatever is before it with the same ease.

This perhaps makes us understand the difference between our way of learning a language and the way in which a child learns it. If the language is a simple one we find it easier to learn and if the language is more complicated we find it harder to learn. For the child it is a matter of indifference whether the language is simple or complicated and whether the language has a few words or many words. It is also a matter of indifference to him whether there is one language in his environment or more. It must not be forgotten that there is a world of difference between a rigid object like a camera and a living human intelligence like the child's. The child, by appropriating to himself and taking possession of a language, builds the foundations and erects the scaffolding for the ever-rising structure of human progress.

9

THE CHILD AND

THE ADULT

Childhood is a period of extraordinary sensitivity. The absorption of impressions, sights, sounds and all other aspects of the environment is all comprehensive and indelible. Facility and spontaneity are the characteristics of the acquisitions of childhood.

The difference between the acquisitions of childhood and the acquisitions of adult life can be understood when one considers the pleasure with which a child masters his mother tongue and the labour with which an adult learns a foreign tongue.

The child achieves perfect results without fatigue. The adult achieves them imperfectly and with laborious efforts. This difference between the child and the adult is not confined to the mastery of language. It extends to many other things of great importance.

Let us take the question of the movements of the body. A child of about two and a half years can stand on his feet. He can walk and run and climb. These abilities were acquired at special periods of development when such development was spontaneous and without willed exertion.

When these abilities are established the adult can start to perfect many of the movements he possesses. He can learn to dance and swim and perform acrobatic feats. But these are things for which he needs an example, a teacher who will tell him step by step, how to do these things. He achieves degrees of skill in these matters through prolonged training and deliberate efforts. It must be remembered that in achieving mastery in the above physical movements the adult is building on the permanent foundation constructed by the child without painful effort and by sheer spontaneous self-activity.

THE CHILD AND THE ADULT

Deliberate effort is associated with adult life. Spontaneous acquisition is the characteristic of childhood. Look at an adult who wants to be an athlete. He has to keep on exercising himself. The pianist must keep on playing the piano. The dancer must keep on dancing. The boxer must keep on boxing. All these activities have to be carried on with persistent and willing effort.

How can this difference between the child and the adult be explained?

We have to fall back on the laws of life. There are certain powers, certain aptitudes in organisms at the early stages of development, which adults do not possess. Beings which are in the process of development pass through certain phases, which are temporary in character and which may be termed creative phases.

During these periods the developing organisms are endowed with special sensitivity and are subject to certain transformations similar to those which are visible in physical growth. It is on account of this sensitivity that the child is capable of taking from the environment and incorporating in himself what he has taken.

Let us take as an example the caterpillar which has special sensitivities during special periods of its life. When the young caterpillar is just out of the egg, it is very sensitive to light and therefore it goes to the end of the branches where light is plentiful and there it finds the tender leaves which form the food suitable to his age. After it has grown it can eat many other things and hence no longer needs the sensitivity to light, and in fact loses that sensitivity.

It must not be thought that when the caterpillar loses its sensitivity to light it becomes blind. It merely loses the special attraction for light which made it go wherever it saw strong light. Though it loses the old sensitivity to light, it probably sees things better than when it was small. We may say that the caterpillar has become indifferent to light after this special period of development is over.

It is the same with human beings. When children are in their sensitive periods they have a great enthusiasm, a remarkable burst of activity. When the sensitive period is over, the child becomes indifferent. That which formerly was a tremendous attraction to him is now just like one of the many things that are around him. When the child is in the sensitive period he is like a living flame consuming and devouring in his activity all that concerns the special sensitivity of his development. When the sensitive periods are over, it is as if a flame has gone out.

Then begins the period when strong determination and strenuous efforts are needed.

But there is a unity in the life of every individual. We shall illustrate this unity by again referring to the development of language. During a specific period the lips and the tongue of the child were moving only to suck milk. Later on certain fibres in the lips and the tongue begin to vibrate in a certain fashion. The vocal chords, which in the earlier period were capable of uttering only cries and shouts, in the following period excel the strings of a musical instrument. Gradually all the parts of the child's mechanism of speech come into play in unison and accord, so that the child is able to pronounce all the delicate intonations and complicated sounds which form a human language.

Language is not an easy matter. There are many muscles which have to act together at the same time. There are involved, in speaking a language, movements of several parts of the tongue; also movements of the vocal chords in a special manner; there are, further, certain movements of the muscles in the cheek. Some muscles have to vibrate sideways; others must vibrate up and down; all have to move in a precise way; and all the movements of all parts must be in harmony. If you have not mastered these co-ordinations and combinations in childhood, you will not be able to do the same with perfection nor with such facility later on in life.

Thus the child lays down foundations. The first two and a half years is a fundamental formative period. From that age up to four and a half years is a period of further elaboration and construction. Further structures and elaborations continue. As the periods of creative activity in the sensitive periods slow down, further development and perfection of the individual are brought about by determined efforts and willed activity. But it is the child, by incorporating in himself all the essential elements of the environment including the mother tongue, that embodies in himself and preserves the special characteristics and genius of the race.

THE CHILD AND THE ADULT

Just imagine how wonderful it would be if adults retained the capacity of the child, who by means of spontaneous activity and without conscious exertion, learns to speak a language with all its complexities! Just imagine that we could become engineers or mathematicians or philosophers in the manner in which the child learns the mother tongue!.

How wonderful it would be if all the sciences came into our brains just with the work of breathing and living and absorbing the environment! At first we would not notice that anything remarkable had happened. Then all of a sudden our acquisitions would twinkle like stars in our heads and we would realize that we did possess them. We would wake up to find that all these possessions were ours without any exertion, without any fatigue.

Does it not sound like a fairy tale? If you were told that there was a planet where there were no teachers, no schools, no necessity for study, where the inhabitants, just by living and going about, knew every subject and all the sciences of the world, you would think that planet was paradise.

That which appears to be imaginary and fantastic is a reality. This is the method of acquisition of knowledge by the child during periods of creative sensitivity. The child's mastery of spoken language and physical movements are examples of this method of acquisition. The adult throughout his life builds the superstructure of knowledge, experience and skill on the foundation laid in childhood.

It has to be emphasized that the powers of the absorbent mind of the child are not confined to the acquisition of language: the absorption extends to all the mental and moral characteristics that are regarded as fixed in humanity or race or community and includes patriotism, religion, social habits, technical dispositions, prejudices and in fact all items that make up the sum-total of human personality. The possibility of the continued duration of the absorbent mind in special adult cases due to interest, concentration or otherwise would provide a subject for a fascinating investigation.

10

LIBERATION FROM THE

PRISON AND THE DESERT

The steps towards development are the steps of freedom. But at the earliest stages the child is virtually in prison. He cannot walk or go where he wants to go. He is incapable of expressing his needs. He cannot feed himself. He is confined to a prison of flesh. When he begins to walk, when he can express his needs, or is able to feed himself, he is becoming independent in those respects.

Thus, growth is a successive breaking of the bonds which hold the child down in dependence upon others. We shall refer later to the necessity of liberating the child from the triple desert of inaction, of boredom, and of repression. For the present we shall deal with what we may call the child's prison life.

A child may be well cared for; may be supplied with a nursery and a nurse; he may be given everything necessary for his physical comforts and needs. But if a mother's affection and attention are absent the child is in prison; he is virtually abandoned. The nursery may be thoroughly disinfected; it may have white walls and a nurse with clean well-starched clothes; and the nurse may strictly follow all the rules of hygiene. Yet, the child is in a walled prison, without the freedom, without the activities needed for his special period of development.

The circumstances described above show that while the body is carefully looked after, it is possible to abandon the soul of the child. Such abandonment is harmful to the character and formation of the child. Just as the neglect of physical hygiene causes physical defects and deviations from normal health, so the neglect of psychic hygiene produces mental faults and deviations from normal conduct.

Here we wish to point out that the defects to which we are referring are not defects which some people say we possess in

38

this life because of sins committed in other lives or because of the original sin of our first parents. The faults and defects which we are speaking of are those which come to human beings because the treatment they have received was a wrong treatment. The ones we are referring to are those which are caused by the wrong conditions which we parents, nurses or modern society, have forced upon the child and on account of which, as a consequence and reaction to which, these defects have arisen.

The defects of children to which we refer are not even due to heredity. They are due to our failure to prepare a suitable environment for the child; due to the attitude of the persons round the child; due to ignorance of the needs of the special periods in the development of a child. The defects are due to inaction and neglect in assisting the child to liberate himself gradually from his prison house.

Thus it comes about that if children happen to be sent to school at three years of age, the general idea is that the business of education is to correct the defects acquired by the child during previous years. When the child goes to the primary school at about six years, the impression is that the task of education is to correct the defects of that age.

It may be presumed on this basis that as one grows bigger and bigger his faults and defects grow bigger in number and more serious in quality and that the task of education is to correct and rectify all those things which are wrong in human nature.

But what happens generally to the child? After his imprisonment in homes where his needs were ignored, where little or no provision was made for the special periods of his development, after further confinement and neglect in the pre-primary school, the child goes to the primary school. The primary school gathers the pilgrims of the desert, herds them together, and regiments them in order to teach them. Already in the pre-primary school the child has been bored without suitable activity and without sufficient opportunity for spontaneous development. The child then arrives at the primary school full of defences and full of defects, like a porcupine full of spines. Having had little opportunity of doing things or of learning things by doing, he is lazy and full of discouragement.

The primary school begins by teaching the child how to write. A hand which had done very little handwork is asked to begin work by taking up a pen and making signs. The child must learn the alphabetical symbols which arouse no interest in him at all. The child gets depressed.

The child has to learn without any interest in his learning. He has to learn against his inclinations and behaves as if he were forced to eat things for which he has no appetite. He feels as if he were a person condemned to forced labour. The teacher is obliged to urge him and compel him by threats or punishments or prizes.

All this places, at the very roots of life, a hatred for work. Such hatred and disinclination to work is fostered and cultivated by the system. It is not an easy thing to eradicate these early associations. These will linger in the child to the great detriment of his life. Contrast the above attitude of the child to work at the above type of school to the joy and spontaneity with which he mastered his mother tongue or learned the movements of his body in the earlier stages. Under the above circumstances the school becomes an arid desert where the child has no suitable food for his appetite, no suitable drink for his thirst, and where he feels lonely, oppressed and unhappy.

The purpose of education must be to prevent defects and faults and to remove in advance the possibility of their occurrence. The main task of education must be similar to the task which in the physical field has been left to hygiene, which is concerned with the prevention of physical illnesses and the maintenance of physical health.

Let us suppose that the child has not been abandoned in the early sensitive periods; that the needs of the child in these special periods were recognized; that conditions and facilities were supplied to the child to develop through self-activity according to natural laws of development; let us suppose that such a child who has received the necessary physical and psychic care comes to our House of Children at about three years of age.

In the House of Children there exists the necessary equipment, facilities and environment necessary to feed and satisfy the psychic appetite of the child. Then, what happens?

The child's natural sensitivity having not been interfered with, the child absorbs the written language in the same manner as it previously absorbed the spoken language: with spontaneity and ease, without fatigue or conscious exertion. He finds joy in his work. His sensitivity is displayed in the enthusiastic efforts he puts forth to accomplish his objectives.

In the earlier period as we already mentioned, the child, in a natural way, exploded into words. Then there was an explosion into sentences. Why cannot there be further explosions? Perhaps in the second period there may be another explosion into writing, an explosion into reading, and other explosions into several aspects of knowledge or skill. If the right conditions are there, what can prevent such phenomena in the child's spontaneous activity?

We have found that in the earlier period when the child exploded into words, the child had a hunger for names of all sorts of objects. Suppose that hunger has increased with the continuation of the sensitive period and the child is still hungry for words and names, nouns and verbs and other significant terms. Suppose we satisfy this natural hunger while it lasts and give the child as large a quantity of words and names as possible. Suppose again if, instead of allowing him to absorb names and words at random, we give the child names and words in groups and in classifications so as to make absorption easier for him.

The question is: What sort of names and words should we place within the child's reach? They may be names of the objects in the environment. They may also be scientific names. One important aspect of science is the systematized terminology applied to objects of Nature.

You may think it difficult for a child of three years to absorb such enormous quantities of scientific terms. It must be remembered that scientific terms are also names of objects in the child's environment. Everything in the world has a name; and to a child hungry for words, all names are welcome, whether scientific or otherwise.

The child absorbs things from the environment. We can place the things and the names in his environment. He absorbs both; directly associates the things with the names; and increases his mastery of things and names, with the facility with which he learnt to speak his mother tongue in the earlier parts of his sensitive period.

When the child is in the sensitive period and has a hunger for names (which is also a hunger for knowledge) you may give him names in biology, botany, geography, physics, zoology or any other science. Give them to him in orderly fashion as accompaniments of the objects or parts of the objects of his environment. He is able to master them as easily as he mastered in the earlier period his physical movements.

This process of re-examination of the objects of the environment and the association of further names with these objects come to the child as a joyful experience and a kind of fascinating discovery. The child has already in the earlier period grasped the whole of the environment. The various parts and aspects of his environment with their names associated with them, now appear to him as if presented under a magnifying glass showing the details of structure and particulars of form.

You may say: This appears to be very rosy; this sort of thing may happen in Utopia; we are here on this hard earth; can you teach the child mathematics in this way?

It has been pointed out by philosophers that the human mind is essentially mathematical. If this is so, provided the necessary materials are to be found in the House of Children, the innate powers of the mind may be awakened and the child of about four and a half years of age may be able to do big sums with figures involving thousands or millions. If these performances are suited to the sensitive period of childhood there is every possibility that the child may explode into figures, as he did in an earlier period explode into words and into sentences, or as he does, under proper care, explode into writing and reading during special periods of his development.

The above shows that the unexpected work done by the child between three and six years of age may anticipate and cover up a considerable part of the work at present done in a primary school consisting of pupils from seven to twelve years of age.

Just imagine a child of seven years entering the primary school knowing how to write and how to read, how to do with accuracy four fundamental operations in arithmetic, knowing the rudiments of the natural sciences and also of geography; you will then realize that such a child should enter a school worthy of his achievement and the stage of development he has reached.

When such a child enters the primary school, if the necessary environments and facilities are given to him, he will carry into that school the joy of activity, the enthusiasm and hunger for knowledge which he displayed in the previous years. Consequently the child will reach in the primary school a degree of development even higher than in the middle school. The same accelerated, intensified and joyful development may be carried higher and higher up to the university stage and beyond.

All that we have been mentioning in the form of suppositions, we have actually observed and experienced in our Houses of Children and primary schools in many parts of the world.

Thus we find that every earlier period is more important than the later period and that we have to go back to the second year or the first year or down to the birth of the child to build better and better foundations for the development of the child. By giving care and attention to the child according to the needs of each special period from the very beginning, and by liberating him from what we have figuratively called the Prison and the Desert, the intelligence of the child will become a great energy, in fact the greatest energy in the world.

11

LEADING THE MARCH OF CIVILIZATION

The magic organism which leads the march of civilization is the child. We shall in this chapter deal with the obstructions to the progress of the child caused unintentionally by those charged with the care of the child. Assistance to the progress of the child, which is identical with the progress of civilization, can be brought about only by means of knowledge of the powers of the child and by penetrating deeper and deeper into the mysteries of childhood. The most astonishing power of man, in comparison to all other orders of creation, is man's adaptability to the ever-changing conditions of his environment and it is by giving the necessary assistance to the child that the upward evolution of mankind and the forward march of civilization can be helped.

The obstruction on the part of those responsible for the care of education of the child comes about in the following way. The cause is really the desire to teach and the reluctance to allow the child to learn. A syllabus of work is there; and the teacher appears to stand in front of the child and to say, "Thus far and no further".

Irrespective of the powers and potentialities of the child, and ignorant of his natural approach to knowledge, the adult prescribes certain forms and contents of knowledge and confines the child to these arbitrary limits. This is obstruction.

 Our concept of education may be figuratively described by saying that the educator stands behind the child and allows him to go forward as far as he can, whereas the other method is to stand in front of the child and prevent him from going further than the limits imposed on him by the teacher.

The consequences of our attitude are worth noting. When the teacher, instead of imposing herself on the mind of the child, sympathetically watches his development, not only does the child learn better but there is an expansion of the personality of the child. We witness, as it were, the freeing of an energy. What is relevant is not the capacity or the brilliance of the teacher. Independently of the teacher the child expands itself. We behold with surprise this energy which previously did not appear to exist and which did not manifest itself.

This method of standing behind the child instead of opposing him, becomes a support to the child and helps the unfolding of his powers. It is like the germination of a seed, or the blossoming of a flower. The energies of the child which are latent, unknown and hidden, reveal themselves and become manifest in concrete action and purposeful achievement.

Education in general pays no heed to these energies, because they are so far away from the syllabus and its narrow contents. The teacher does not understand the existence of these energies or is indifferent about them. The energies thus remain latent and for practical purposes remain as if they were non-existent.

The first task of education should be to help this expansion and remove obstructions to such expansion. That which is in nature must be treasured by education. To do so, what is in nature must be discovered. We must see what nature can give us. After seeing the powers and energies which nature can give us, we must help the expansion of these powers and energies.

Then we must go above nature. Man can go above nature. When man controls and utilizes the powers of nature he is above nature. The march of civilization is marked by man's increasing mastery of the powers of nature and his use of them for the service of mankind.

But if you take away the help which nature gives, if you obstruct the expansion of natural powers, how can the child be anything but poorer than what he is by nature? The child can be above nature. He can be supranatural. The supranatural must be built on the natural. If we want to go beyond nature, if we want to supersede nature, we must base ourselves upon nature and treasure all the contributions nature has to make to us.

If we say the clock must be above the table so that you may see it, what is necessary is not only to have the clock but also the table; if there were no table, the clock must disappear below the plane of your vision.

WHAT YOU SHOULD KNOW ABOUT YOUR CHILD

To be able to go beyond nature, to build upon nature, we must penetrate the secrets of nature. We must delve into the mysteries of that period of childhood when the child is unable to tell us what is taking place. We must interpret nature and learn her ways. We must then give every help to the child in all matters which appear to be his natural needs.

We shall now refer to the progress of civilization. We have already stated that the intelligence of the child properly developed is the greatest energy in the world. This intelligence leads the march of civilization through two great instruments, human language and human hands.

We have already pointed out that language is an instrument of human intelligence and that language is necessary for progress. When men have to accomplish big tasks of civilization, it is not individuals but communities that do so. In order to be able to accomplish their work, communities have to understand each other and in order to co-ordinate their work, they have to understand those ideas which other individuals or communities have put forward. Without such mutual understanding and intercommunication through language the great feats of civilization cannot be carried out.

When a plan is approved and accepted how is it carried out? Human hands carry it out. The performance of mighty enterprises are due to human hands. Human individuals moving in so many ways, talking in various languages, and working with their hands in co-operation and combination, impelled by their intelligence, constitute the picture of human advancement and civilization.

There is a resemblance between the movement of human progress and the physical movement of human beings. It is true that animals are capable of movement but there is an infinite difference between man and animals.

Man walks by putting one foot in front of the other. Animals do the same. Certain animals are able to run as soon as they are born. Man also does this sometime later. Man's movements, however, are not confined to the unchanging movements of the animals. There is incredible progress in the modes and methods of even his physical movements.

Man can run like the deer and the rabbit. He can jump like the frog or the kangaroo. By practice and training man is capable of a variety of movements like dancing, wrestling and boxing which cannot be equalled by animals. By the application of his intelligence and by co-operative effort man has gone very much further.

If we review the march of civilization we see that there is no animal that can run as fast as man when he travels in a train or an automobile; that no animal can dig as deep as man when he goes into the depths of his coal mines; and that there is no bird of the sky that can fly faster and higher than when man flies in his aeroplane.

What is all this due to? Behind all these performances of man is his intelligence which has at its service two hands. It is the hands of man directed by his intelligence that built the train and the automobile; that dug the coal mines to the depth of so many miles; that shaped the aeroplane and made the engine that moves it at such a tremendous speed. It is impossible to describe the infinite number of things which man has done in the past and which he will do in the future with his hands.

We cannot say that man as an individual can do all the things that individual animals can do. Nor can we compare man with all the animals and say: "Here is the greatest of all animals." The fact is that if all the abilities of all animals were added together, the sum total would be merely the starting point of man's powers.

What is most surprising in man is that his evolution never ends but always continues. It is true that at present man has reached a high degree of evolution. He speaks across the oceans. He sees through immensities of space. He flies around the terrestrial globe. He can not only do so many things which were thought to be beyond the realm of possibility but he has created such a world by the exercise of his intelligence that the world is no longer the world it was.

Certainly the human being of today enters into an environment which is vastly different from the environment of the human child of ten thousand years ago. We can ask ourselves: "Will this child, who after fifteen months of striving, is hardly able to hold himself on his feet, manage to adapt himself to such a complicated environment?" Yet it is true that the child adapts himself to the enormous amount of inventions and innovations of the new world of today with the same ease as the human child of ten thousand years ago adapted himself to the simple environment of that time.

This wonderful power of adaptation is a remarkable power of childhood. The child goes about with the same ease and the same tranquillity no matter at what level of civilization he is born. As he imbibed his home language, however complicated it was, with the same ease just by moving about on his two tiny feet, he adapts himself to any environment however complicated it is.

Life is so advanced today and is so fast advancing that if we came back to earth after ten thousand years, we might say that we would not like to live in such times as those. Did not our grandmothers say: "I do not like these new-fangled ideas of modern days"? Yet ten thousand years hence, the children will adapt themselves to the new environment with the same spontaneity as children of primitive days adapted themselves to their primitive environments.

The progress of civilization is similar to the varieties of movements in man. Man stands erect on his feet; he jumps, runs, and is able to produce the rhythm and harmony which constitute a graceful dance. Such movements were scarcely possible in a child.

Are we to think that when an adult wishes to become a dancer, a special set of muscles are suddenly created? Or when a man weaves a fine web of lace or when he produces a beautiful miniature or delicate piece of art, are we to think that a number of suitable muscles are created at the appropriate moment to enable him to perform the minute and delicate movements necessary to produce those masterpieces? No, the muscles were always there. They were there many centuries ago; and they will be there centuries hence ready to do whatever there is to be done.

The fact that a man always makes new things and new inventions militates against the idea of mere heredity. If it were heredity, man would just do what his forefathers had done. But the medium of transmission of the innate powers of mankind from generation to generation is the child. The child is the means of evolution and we must give him the necessary assistance to put him in contact with the environment in which he is born and to put in vibration those mysterious fibres of brain, nerve and muscle so that they may work in obedience to the will and intelligence of the child.

All the infinite potentialities of man indicating an increasing progress from generation to generation are contained in the child. The energies and powers embodied in a tiny little child are more powerful than the newly discovered energy of the atom.

More research and more investigation are wanted to discover the mysteries and hidden powers of the child and to help him to utilize them for the service of man than for the utilization of atomic or other energies. For man's mind which directs and controls energy is, without question, superior to all the forces it can control. It is by leading the child to the fullest development of his powers that we can help the child to lead the continued march of human civilization.

12

THE HAPPINESS OF
ACHIEVEMENT

One test of the correctness of educational procedure is the happiness of the child itself. For a growing organism growth itself is happiness. The growth of the child is by means of activity. Activity according to vital laws of development is happiness.

Rest or inaction is foreign to the child's nature. What motivates activity is interest. The urges of nature in special periods of the child's life provide the interest. The joy of the child is the joy of achievement.

The child loves to achieve a complete unit of activity. The achievement, however trivial to the adult, gives a sense of power and independence to the child. When he has completed a special unit or cycle of activity, the accomplishment makes him happy. The accompanying hedonic element seems to encourage him to further and further activity in the way of self-development. One is forced to remember Aristotle's statement to the effect that happiness is activity in the way of perfect excellence.

We shall give a few striking examples of children's spontaneous achievement at different stages of development. The following examples will show the happiness which the child feels in adventures into the field of achievement and also will demonstrate the necessity of giving the child the help and special environments which will allow him to develop with safety and without danger.

We shall give an example to show how already the child at a very early stage is happy even with incipient activity. When a child of four months is lying on his stomach, he raises up his head and tries to elevate his shoulders. Later when he tries to sit up he grabs at things around him so that he may sit up more quickly.

THE HAPPINESS OF ACHIEVEMENT

At this stage it is a great help to the child if we allow him to grasp our fingers or hands or whatever object he is trying to hold. In this way we help him in his earliest set of movements. Even these little movements make him happy in relation to his age.

At about ten months of age the child begins to understand his environment. He becomes aware of the relative position of the objects which surround him. At this time there is a great need of giving the child suitable objects to enable him to gather the necessary experience. The effort of the adult should be, after providing the articles, to see that certain objects are always in the same place. The attention of the child may be skilfully drawn as to whether an object is on top of another or below it; or whether it is to the right or to the left; and whether it is far from or close to another object. This shows how early education can begin.

Here is another example of the happiness of the child in achievement. In a house in London leading from one floor to another there was a staircase which was very steep. It was well covered first with canvas and then with a soft carpet. A small child of about one year began to go up this staircase. Everyone present tried to stop him from doing it but the child appeared determined to see the end of his exercise. This small child who was still almost going on four legs instead of two, went all the way up the staircase. He was so tiny that he had to climb by putting himself sideways and by first putting one leg and then the other leg. It was a tremendous athletic exercise. When the child came to the top of the staircase he was satisfied with this exercise. Probably he felt he no longer needed to be careful. So, he turned round and tumbled down all the way to the bottom of the staircase.

The people watching the performance ran to the child and picked him up and found fault with him saying: "See what you have done". They did not realize the proportions of the child and the staircase. If we fall down a staircase we are so tall that each step gives us a hit; and our weight is so great that each hit is an injury. The child had little weight; so he just kept rolling down the soft carpet. When he found himself seated at the bottom of the staircase, he sat up and smiled and did not worry about what people said. The child was not scared at all.

The only thing he felt was the happiness of having accomplished something by his own efforts. Probably he must also have been happy in having arrived down so quickly.

If you observe a group where there are children of two years of age you will find that those little ones are fond of putting things in order. They spot an object which is out of its place and they put it back in its proper place. We shall now describe a true event to show some children's aversion to disorder.

A little girl of three was taking dancing lessons under a tutor. This three year old had a younger brother who was eighteen months old. The teacher was playing on the piano and the girl was learning simple steps. The small child showed great interest in these movements. It was decided that as the little boy was interested in the lessons in dancing he should take part in the next lesson.

When the teacher arrived on the following day the small child refused to go for the lesson but started to cry. The people in the house said: "It is absurd to make a child of this age do these exercises." "Do you not see", they said, "he does not want to do them?" The fact was different.

The child was angry because the teacher's hat had been put on the top of a chair. He threw himself against the hat and said, "Hat rack. Hat rack". What the child meant was that the hat should not be on the chair but should be on the hat rack. After the hat had been placed upon the hat rack the child was ready for his lesson and began to walk to the music round the table.

As an example of the child's desire to accomplish a cycle of activity and to feel the joy of achievement, we shall describe an event which could have taken place only in a Montessori House of Children. The children of one of our Houses of Children were being fed on a lawn outside. A child of one and a half years of age had made up her mind to carry to the lawn a very long loaf of bread. The loaf was longer than the child. In order to carry it the child had to throw herself back, put her arms round the loaf and walk without being able to see the ground upon which her two unsteady feet were treading.

What would be the natural instinct of an adult under these circumstances? If this event did not take place in a Montessori House of Children, the weight would have been removed from the child. But she was allowed to carry it. She crossed a whole lawn, walking on the grass which is more difficult to walk on than ordinary ground; and she brought this big loaf without being able to look down on the ground, all the way across to the table where the loaf was to be cut in order to feed the children.

The sight was interesting to see. The child's dog was following her and was looking at the child with great interest. The adults who were there followed the child with rapt attention ready to give any assistance required. Luckily no one interfered: neither the dog nor the two ladies who were looking after the children. The greatest joy of the child was in having accomplished this cycle of activity through her own effort and being able to say "I have done it".

Once Dr. Montessori found herself alone with a child of one and a half years. The maid of the house had ironed some napkins and had put them, one on top of the other, in a pile. There were twenty well-starched and ironed napkins. The child took one of these napkins and carried it to the opposite corner of the room. Very carefully he laid it on the ground. Then back he came to the pile and with the same care took a second napkin. Almost following the same straight line he went to the place where he had laid the first napkin and placed the second napkin on the first napkin. Fortunately there was nobody to stop his cycle of activity. Dr. Montessori wanted to see how long the child would go on with this exercise.

He took the twenty napkins one by one; and made twenty trips and built a pile of twenty napkins at the other corner of the room. Perhaps you may say the child might have said, "It is finished" and stopped his exercise.

As soon as the pile was made in the corner of the room, the child picked up the first napkin and walked back and put it on top of the table again. One after another he made twenty trips again and carried the twenty napkins from the corner back to the table with the same care and seriousness as before. The second pile on the table was not in too much disorder. When the maid came back she would certainly wonder what had happened to the napkins; but luckily the maid was not there.

There is no doubt the child was happy at having completed a cycle of activity. You can imagine how often a child is prevented from carrying out such exercises so conducive to his happiness and so necessary for his development. It must be remembered that such activity not only makes a child happy but also makes him even-tempered.

We should point out that as these experiments are impossible to carry out in the homes of children for various reasons, it becomes necessary to create institutions like our Houses of Children in which the child will find the means and equipment which are suitable for these cycles of experience. Some of these items of equipment are wooden houses specially built with staircases leading up to trees which children may climb in safety.

One cycle of activity provided in our Houses of Children has become almost a classic and a favourite theme for photographers. There is a picture taken in one of our schools in Berlin before the war. This picture represents a child of two holding a plate with one hand and in the position of going round with a piece of cloth in order to clean and dry the plate. The picture also shows four older children of about three and a half years of age standing at a low window just above the head of the child, looking with rapt attention at the little baby's performance.

It gladdens one's heart to see the bright expression in the face of the little child and the attitude of concentration in his demeanour. It is still more delightful to see the joy and satisfaction and absorbing interest with which the older children are watching the little child below. A new life seems to dawn on the child, a new confidence in himself, a new dignity born out of a new victory and a new achievement. Equally impressive is its effect on the onlookers.

We shall conclude by referring to a princess of Holland who on her second birthday was presented to the public some years ago. All the newspapers in Holland published her picture; and in what form did they present it? They showed a picture of the princess holding in one hand a plate and in the other hand a towel with which she was cleaning a plate. Gladness and satisfaction seemed to light up the countenance of the little princess; for, a unit of purposeful work well achieved is an uplifting experience and a source of happiness.

13

THE KEY TO MENTAL HEALTH

AND GROWTH

We have seen how necessary for the development of the child are the performance of various cycles of activity and what are called experiences on the environment. The basic principle is that the mind should grip reality and establish contacts with reality suitable to every stage of development. Personal experiences carried out on reality form real knowledge. Such experiences are not only the basis of mental growth but also of mental health.

Every stage of development influences all succeeding stages. What is of great importance in one level goes into oblivion at the next level; and something else acquires importance. The task of education is to supply the needs of every stage from the beginning.

The failure to provide facilities for the performance of the cycles of activity and the experiences on the environment suitable to the various stages of development destroys the conditions of normality; the child must function in the manner which nature dictates: if he does not do so, or if he is prevented from functioning normally as nature dictates, he becomes abnormal.

Two evil consequences follow. First there is an interference with the growth of the child. This interference affects all succeeding stages. The second evil consequence is the interference with the mental health of the child. This interference also may be permanent.

The interruption of cycles of activity produces certain inner conditions in the mind of the child which deprive him of self-confidence and neutralize his ability to finish what he has started. When a child is continuously interrupted while fulfilling cycles of activity, the child is gradually losing the courage, the constancy and the determination necessary for achievement.

In later years he is charged with unsteadiness, want of determination or lack of perseverance. These defects are taken as characteristics of certain children. The fact is they are not so. They are the consequence of the interruptions of the child's normal cycles of activity in earlier years.

Particularly in the case of a child healthy and psychically robust, there is a tendency to be continuously on the move. Not having been provided with an environment that could motivate cycles of activity, or having been regularly interrupted in cycles of activity which he had begun, the child fails to acquire a habit of applying himself to purposeful ends; his courage has been reduced and his self-confidence undermined.

Then, at a later stage a strong healthy child who has been either neglected or repressed comes to school, the adults say: "He starts many things, but he cannot finish them. As soon as he has started one thing he stops it and goes to something else." The child is not to be blamed. Nature is not to be blamed. It is education or better want of education that is responsible for the above defects of the child. The urge and impulse placed by nature in the child to perform certain cycles of activity were obstructed and repressed. The consequences are the defects.

The baneful effects of repression and of the prevention of a child from accomplishing spontaneously tasks suited to the various stages of his development may be described as follows: The child develops a subconscious attitude in which he seems to say, "If I start to do something, somebody is going to stop me; therefore I won't start it." Thus not only a lack of persistence as shown above is developed but, as a corollary, the child develops inattention, fearfulness, hesitancy and indecision.

These defects almost forced on the child through want of care or want of knowledge, may accompany him through all the successive periods of life. The defects undermine character and we meet with individuals who seem to be always in doubt and appear to be asking themselves for the major part of the day: "Shall I do it or not do it?"

This indecision permeates the mind of a person so much that sometimes it is reflected in his speech. You find people who wait and pause for words and who do not know what words to use. Their difficulty is not that they lack words, but they lack the decision as to which word they are going to use. In some cases when indecision and fear are at their highest, they begin to stammer and stutter. In extreme cases they are dumb and can scarcely open their mouth. These and many other defects can be traced back to repression in childhood.

The harmful effects of repression have to be examined further. The repressed child has an abiding fear that somebody is going to interrupt or prevent his undertaking. He loses the courage necessary for accomplishment. This fosters timidity which develops into a state of pathological anxiety. He wishes to accomplish an activity. He has the capacity to accomplish it, but he has reached such a state of mind that he does not even attempt it. The child suffers from a consciousness of inferiority which modern thinkers call an inferiority complex.

An inferiority complex is loss of inner strength of the mind. It is a distressing mental state in a child as if the child had lost what he once possessed. It must be remembered that the timidity that is produced by repression is not based on reality. It is not anything positive and real, like the fear of a snake, or a tiger, or the fear of falling down and hurting oneself. It is an inner mental condition similar to a permanemt nightmare. It is a deviation from normality. It obstructs and incapacitates the child for life.

Adults augment this state of mind by obtaining obedience by threatening the child and introducing into his mind unreal fears. These fears lead to deviations from normality; for the fears so introduced are not based on reality. The fear of darkness, for example, is a phantom fear; normally a child is not afraid of darkness.

We shall give an example: A child of eighteen months used to sleep in a bed which was built by us in such a manner that he could get up by himself and did not wait for somebody else to take him out of the cage in which children are usually put to sleep. This bed was on the ground floor; all the windows opened on to the garden; and for fear of intrusion by animals or human beings the windows were firmly shut every night. Thus the rooms at night were absolutely dark.

The above mentioned child woke up early one morning while the other people were asleep. He went through three of the rooms which were full of beds and other furniture. Although he was repeatedly saying to himself, "It is dark and I am going to fall," he did not stop from crossing the three rooms which were completely dark.

The difference between this child whose education did not put into his mind fears of fantasy and others who were made to develop a mental abnormality may be seen from the behaviour of two elder sisters of this child. These two elder sisters who were about thirteen and fourteen years of age respectively, every time there was a thunderstorm at night were frightened and scared and shrieked with fear. Once this little boy of three years of age went over to console them during a storm and said: "It is nothing."

Examples may be multiplied to show that this fear is not a natural fear in the child. We have seen another little child who woke up early in the morning while it was still dark and ran to the door to meet the milkman, received the milk and carried it to the kitchen. There was no fear of darkness in that child.

Some children coming to our Houses of Children have these defects. The energies of the child, whose natural tendency was to go outside, in pursuit of exercise and experiences, seem to have turned inward and to be buried in the child. Some children do not know how to apply their hands to any purposeful activity. There is, however, plenty of unused energy in their hands and limbs.

The inability to develop an orderly activity and consequent disorderly movement produce a disorderly mind or a confused mind. The confused mind may be vivacious; but it is a vivacity without a purpose or aim.

Hence the difference between true imagination based on true images or ideas derived from reality and false imagination based on fancies and fantasies without any bearing on reality. True imagination forms an important part of human intelligence; but false imagination consists of disorderly movements of the mind.

When a person's mind which has not organized itself wanders into fantasy, having detached itself from reality, his hands, coming in contact with the surrounding objects, spoil them and put them in disorder. Indeed one of the characteristics of children of the strong type, who have not organized their minds or movements, is to get angry. Three things go together: disorderly minds, disorderly movements and anger.

THE KEY TO MENTAL HEALTH AND GROWTH

Such children are dangerous. The cause is the failure to create an environment in the earlier stages to enable the children to carry out experiences and go through cycles of activity which would have steadied them and created harmony between mind and body by contacts with reality.

But just imagine a young teacher left suddenly in the midst of fifteen children who throw things away, break things down, fight and slap one another. The teacher needs plenty of knowledge, tact and patience to tackle the problem. We have seen a strong man of excellent health who begged for assistance when he was put to teach music to forty little "angels".

We are concerned with the small child in the constructive period. For the sake of the child's mental health and efficiency as a future worker, his mind must be developed in close contact with reality and by means of practical exercises. Normal development excludes fantasy and erratic movements of the mind divorced from reality. Sanity, balance and mental health are conditioned by harmony with the external world.

We may at this stage refer to adults who have erratic minds, who cannot fix their attention on what is told to them, who cannot work with constancy and who become easily angry. Such people have lost touch with reality. They are called abnormal or insane persons. Such people in their thinking and acting behave like runaway horses.

What is the cure? In the olden days crazy people were tied to beds in what were called straight-jackets. Another cure was to put them during attacks of fury under a cold shower so as to take away the heat of their body and their brains. It was also a practice to give them opium or other drugs which made them sleep and calmed the nerves.

Today, in cases which are curable, the cure is to interest the mind in some work or activity which will put it back in relation with reality. The idea is that since the deviation or abnormality is due to detachment from reality, the cure is to hook it back, as it were, to reality again. As an example, in the case of melancholia which makes people continually sad and disappointed, some activity or some purposeful work seems to animate and vivify the person and cure the disease.

The principle which we are trying to emphasize is the following: that the mind should be connected with reality and

59

that such a connection is the fundamental basis of not only mental health but also of mental development. Our reference to insane or unbalanced persons was to make you recognize the difference between, on the one hand, a false imagination consisting of fancies and fantasies due to absence of contact with reality and on the other hand the true imagination of the great scientists, the true mystic, the creative poet and the dramatist whose ideas and thoughts have been derived by direct contact with reality. What we as educators have to prevent is the disorderly wandering of an unhealthy and disorderly mind. What we have to foster in our House of Children is the co-ordinated movement of body and mind in contact with reality.

14

THE CAMERA AND THE

CRYSTAL

We have already pointed out that obstruction of the child's normal cycles of activity creates certain defects which may continue for life. Some writers call such obstructions by the name of repressions; they also call the consequent defects by the name of complexes.

It must be noted that physical illustrations about mental functions are merely illustrations and do not exactly describe what goes on invisibly in the mind. Physical illustrations are only an assistance to understanding mental phenomena.

When we say that at certain stages of life the child's mind absorbs the environment as easily as the sensitive plate of the camera records scenes and sights, we are merely pointing out a similarity.

In the same way when we say that just as a saturated solution must be kept still and unmoved so that crystals of perfect shape may be formed, in like manner an inner mental calm and absence of disturbance are necessary for the settling down of accurate ideas in the mind, we are again referring to a similarity which is helpful to understand what really happens in the mind.

Supposing a saturated solution is not allowed to be still and quiet but is moved and shaken, then what happens? Either the crystals will not be formed or the shaking and the movement may deform the crystals, or break them to pieces or produce distorted crystals.

In the same way unless a sensitive plate or a sensitive film on which a picture has been taken is developed carefully in the coolness or quietness of the cameraman's developing chamber, the picture will be blurred, distorted, mis-shapen or will deviate from reality.

The formation of defects of character or defects of thinking caused by obstruction to a child's performance of normal cycles of activity is similar to the malformation of crystals or the distortion of photographic pictures as described above. On account of the harmful association of ideas, repressions produce complexes which unfortunately may be life-long deviations from normality.

We shall now give some occurrences of childhood to show how impressions are gathered, how ideas are formed and how the resistance or assistance of adults affects the child's development adversely or beneficially.

A small child once placed his dusty shoes on a silk coverlet which was new and beautiful. The person who was looking after the child was annoyed and took the shoes off the coverlet and said: "This is dirty." She then cleaned the coverlet on which the shoes had been placed.

Thenceforward whenever the child saw a pair of shoes, lying on the floor he looked at the shoes and said "dirty" and then went to the sofa or bed and continued rubbing it as if to rub something off. Some automatic mechanism had fixed itself in the mind of the child; the sight of the shoes on the floor was associated with an inevitable impulse to clean the coverlet on the bed or the sofa.

This incident shows that a strong impression received by the child may leave traces for a long time and produce most unexpected reactions. To prevent such deviations the only method will be to provide conditions and environments where repression is avoided.

Here is another case to show how a repression affects the mind of the child. A three year old child was living in a house situated in a garden. The garden had a spouting fountain. The fountain was able to throw long arches of water when the tap was open. The child loved seeing the water coming out of the spouting fountain. He knew where the tap was and how to turn it.

One day with a view to making the spouting fountain play, the child went near the tap and tried to open it. When he was about to open the tap his mother rushed up to him and pulled his hand away from the tap. This repression had such an effect on the child that ever afterwards even when the mother told him to open the tap and nobody else objected, the child would put his hand on the tap and would quickly remove it as if somebody had forced him to do so. It was not possible to make the child complete the operation of opening the tap and making the fountain play.

We may mention another occurrence in one of our Houses of Children in Holland. There was a child of about three years of age who though exhausted after work or exercise would not sit in any of the chairs. The chairs in the House of Children were beautifully painted and very attractive. But the child invariably refrained from making use of any of them.

It was later discovered that this child when she was younger had sat on a chair which had been newly painted and the inmates of the house had said: "Oh! What have you done? You have spoilt your beautiful new dress by sitting on the newly painted chair." Since that time the child had been unable to sit except on a special chair to which she was accustomed. It was noticed that the more brilliantly painted a chair was, the more reluctant the child was to approach it. The problem that we have to face is how to correct the child without causing deviation from normality as above.

The pathological fears or phobias seen in the case of neurasthenia are of similar origin. These are like distorted crystals or mis-shapen camera pictures. As an example of a phobia we may mention a lady of our acquaintance who was afraid of hens. Whenever she saw a hen she appeared to be scared to death. It was clearly a complex in her mind. The lady used to reason with herself often and expressed her belief that her fear was stupid. But the fear persisted and never disappeared.

There are other people who are afraid of remaining in a closed room. There are still others who before going to bed search all over the house to make sure that there are no cats in the house. They know quite well that there are no cats in the house, but they make a careful search. After the search sometimes if they feel nervous they search the house over again to see whether the first search was done correctly; though they know that they have looked very carefully round the house, they do the searching two or three times.

Though such people know that there is no reason for the fear, the fear persists and lingers. There are persons who are terrified of walking in the water. Probably when they were children they were violently reprimanded for playing with water. These complexes are like scratches made upon a sensitive film and remain indelible. We have already pointed out that the avoidance of these complexes can be brought about by providing the child with mental calm and quietness and an absence of sudden interruptions or emotions that may disturb the settling down of ideas. Care, knowledge and vigilance of the person in charge and the absence of danger in the environment are essential requirements. Given the necessary conditions the absorption, even of difficult ideas, is astonishing.

Here is another example. In order to make a certain child comfortable and to prevent it from falling, two cushions were put on a chair and over the cushions there was spread a piece of cloth on which were painted heads of little children, flowers and angels with wings, all in the form of a suitable design. The child was small and hardly able to sit up. But he was observing the flowers and the children on the sheet of cloth.

All of a sudden the child threw himself on a part of the cloth which was raised up by one of the two cushions and began to kiss the faces of the children on the cloth; and then he moved on to the flowers and went on smelling them.

It is usual for parents or relatives in the country where the above incident took place to kiss a child when meeting it. Probably the above child thought it was a matter of course to kiss the face of a child when he saw it. Probably having seen people putting flowers to the nose to inhale the perfume as people often do, it is clear the child, seeing the flowers, thought it a matter of course to smell them.

But one thing worthy of notice was that the above child did not smell the children instead of the flowers nor kiss the flowers instead of the children. He applied his lips to the faces of the children and kissed the faces; then he proceeded to apply his nose to the flowers and sniffed the flowers.

It may be asked whether it is advisable to stop the child from kissing the pictures of babies or smelling pictures of flowers. The child's knowledge is developed by a series of personal discoveries and the child is enough of a realist to discover differences. It is therefore far better to allow the child to discover by himself which are real babies and which are pictures; and which are real flowers and which are their shadows.

We must point out what the nurse of the above child did. When she discovered that the child was fond of smelling even pictures of flowers, she collected all sorts of articles having some smell or other and gave them to the child to sniff as long as he liked. Probably the nurse was anxious to teach the child the difference between actual things and their pictorial representations.

The nurse's anxiety was unnecessary. The differences will settle down and clearness of thoughts and images will follow if the inner calm and quietness of the child's mind are left undisturbed. The above also may be regarded as a case of shaking up the saturated solution and interfering with the process of crystallization; or scratching the sensitive film or preventing a clear picture from being developed in stillness and silence.

To show the necessity of calmness and quiet for the mind to develop correct ideas or elements of knowledge, we wish to mention another example.

Once Dr. Montessori went into a garden full of beautiful flowers, some of them with brilliant colours. There in the garden was a child of about one and a half years of age. The child was alone and Dr. Montessori heard the child laughing loud and with great gusto. Dr. Montessori went near her to find out what was the cause of the child's merriment.

The child was seated on a heap of bricks and intently looking and observing something which Dr. Montessori could not see. As soon as she saw Dr. Montessori, with great delight and enthusiasm, she pointed out to this interested visitor an extraordinarily small and almost invisible insect. This was the object of the child's intense study and the source of his vociferous delight. You can imagine how easy it was to have disturbed the child's minute examination and spontaneous gathering of precise knowledge direct from Nature.

At another time, Dr. Montessori saw a child in a field filled with flowers; but ignoring the flowers, the child was busy pulling out varieties of herbs. Dr. Montessori became interested and remained quiet till the child of his own accord showed her that each herb he had plucked out from the field had a different smell.

These herbs were growing among the grass. The child had separated them from the flowers and grass and was concentrating his mind on the various scents given out by his collection of herbs. Dr. Montessori was astonished at the minute differences of smell which the child was able to make out.

Thus repression is easy but preparing an environment for normal healthy development of the child is difficult. Mental health and mental development depend on the absence of complexes and on making provision for the highest development of every aspect of the child.

We have mentioned the behaviour of the sensitive plate of the camera and the process of crystallization of saturated solutions not only as illustrations but also as caution against any interference with the spontaneous development of the child gathering ideas and elements of knowledge from reality. We wish to repeat that the mind always transcends matter; and that the similarities we have pointed out hold good only in one respect in relation to the mind. The behaviour of material things like the camera or the crystal cannot adequately portray the marvellous processes going on in a mind controlled and activated by an infinite intelligence.

Qualities like strength of will, the capacity for self-creation and the determination to achieve an aim in spite of difficulties found in a human person cannot be associated with mechanical or material things.

15

OBSERVATION AND

DISCOVERY

Before the age of two and a half years the child is almost completely engrossed in the development of his own personality. He has very little communion even with other persons of his own age. After two and a half years of age the child gets interested in other persons; he becomes sociable.

There is another characteristic of the period following two and a half years of age; the child begins to observe more closely and discovers in greater detail the objects of his environment.

Consequently between two and a half years and three years it is advisable to take educative action in two directions. First, as preparation for further development in the House of Children, the social life of the child may be initiated by helping the child to receive visits from people he knows and to make calls on other persons of his acquaintance and thus to enlarge and increase his social contacts as far as he can.

The other preparation for the child of two and a half years is to help him in his more detailed observation and discovery of his environment. This is best done at this stage by providing for long walks for the child.

It has been thought that small children, even when they have begun to walk, cannot walk much. For this reason the perambulator is used to carry children even after they have learnt to walk. Years of experience show that children can walk for miles.

Many a mother says: "I cannot take the child for a walk because the child refuses to go; and when forced to do so, the child cries and is obstinate."

The reason for this trouble is the incorrect procedure adopted.

WHAT YOU SHOULD KNOW ABOUT YOUR CHILD

The consent of the child must be won before the walk. The child must know in his own way that he is going for a walk and where he is going. If you have told the child that you are going for a walk to a certain place you must not change your mind and take the child to some other place. The child must be given a chance to prepare his mind for what is to follow. It is of importance for the development of the child that the child should visualize with as much clearness as is possible under the circumstances, what are going to be his future actions. The visualization or the anticipation in relation to a future event adds a charm and a brightness to the coming event. This advance preparation for what is to follow will not only give the child anticipated pleasure but will make the realization more profitable.

If for instance you intend to have a picnic during a walk it is good to tell the child that you are going to have a picnic; you may let him see how you prepare the picnic basket; you may also let the child help you in all other preparations so that his interest in the coming event may be increased. The important point is that the plan of the walk or the course of it should not be changed without getting the consent of the child. It is of educative value that a child sees a plan and sees it carried out.

Walking in the educative sense is not mere locomotion by putting one foot in front of the other. It is not even physical exercise for the sake of mere exercise. What tires the child is the mechanical walking from one place to another as the fancy of the adult directs him. A walk in the educative sense must have a mental objective, a psychic end.

It must be remembered that at this stage a walk is not intended to make a child walk about. He must be regarded as an observer or an explorer who walks spontaneously for the sake of observation or exploration. It is the child's interest in the outer environment that must determine the course of his walk. The mind moves towards what is of interest; the body follows; and as the mind of the child carries the body about, the physical energy of the child, in the course of such walks, instead of being diminished, appears to be augmented. Thus after miles of such educative walk the child shows no symptoms of excessive fatigue.

OBSERVATION AND DISCOVERY

The principle underlying these walks of the child is as follows: It is not the adult who takes the child for a walk. It is the child who goes for a walk and is accompanied by the adult.

This is what happens. The child goes for a walk. He sees something interesting; and he stops to observe it. If he is sufficiently interested he probably sits down to look at it. The adult's business is to follow the child and to protect it.

We have personally observed a child of two years of age who had gone for a walk and who sat down for a quarter of an hour to observe a donkey eating grass. In like manner supposing the child takes a few steps and seeing a worm is interested in it, he may stop to look at it. He must be allowed to do so. If he is walking up a hill and sees a beautiful sight and stops to look at the panorama, let him do so.

Often small children show interest in things which are not attractive or impressive to us. We have already said that the child is an observer and an explorer. In the earlier stages he has absorbed the major outlines and the more attractive features of his surroundings. At this stage he is interested in greater detail and less impressive things such as a worm or a snail. Thus the child first observes one object and then another, and passing from one place of interest to another he can walk for miles and miles. The environment appears to invite the child to go onward and onward as his interests direct him.

From this it follows that the adult should be educated to follow the child and his interest and to be patient at this continuous interruption of what he calls a walk. To follow the child and help him is really the task of an educator.

Once on a long road outside San Francisco, in California, in one of the suburbs, Dr. Montessori observed a Japanese walking with his child. The child was walking slowly. Usually children like to run; but this child was walking slowly. The steps of the father were set to the pace of the child and he was following the child. All of a sudden the child got hold of the father's trousers. Dr. Montessori was walking behind and was curious to see what would happen. The father merely kept standing with his legs wide open. The child began to run round the legs of his father. The father stood patiently but seriously until the child had finished this sort of game. When the child began to walk again the father went slowly after the child.

WHAT YOU SHOULD KNOW ABOUT YOUR CHILD

Dr. Montessori followed them most interestedly. After a while the child sat down on the side walk; and the father sat near him quietly. How true it is also that in a state of nature a parent or guardian knows intuitively the needs of a child! And how often civilization wipes out this correct impulse and attitude towards a child!

Allowing the child to observe, to explore and to follow his normal interests is a form of respect towards the child. It is an inspiration due to parental love or natural affection.

There are instincts that guide growth. These instincts are placed in man for the protection of the species. If the innate wisdom which nature has given for the care of the young is taken away then a crisis must arise. If the instincts placed in man for his growth and development are weakened or reduced, then something superior must be substituted for them.

Contacts with Nature, observation and exploration of Nature are necessary for the formation of correct ideas and the acquisition of real knowledge. The walks which we have suggested may take place in a park or a field or a forest as well as in the city square or the market. They will to some extent supply the deficiencies caused by the new conditions of civilization. The prepared conditions in our Houses of Children constitute a plan for allowing the child to develop according to natural laws.

True knowledge is direct knowledge of reality and at every stage of progress it is necessary to refer back to Nature to test and verify facts and knowledge. Going back to Nature reawakens and resuscitates those instincts and impulses which are there for the protection of the species.

Yet if civilization is to advance, it is not possible for large numbers of people to go back to Nature permanently. Civilization causes social conditions which take people away from Nature. In fact civilization is a conquest of Nature.

It is not possible for a city worker to give up his business or occupation merely to take his child back to Nature. There must be progress over the simple natural life. There must, however, be provision for the child to have contact with Nature; to understand and appreciate the order, the harmony and the beauty in Nature; and also to master the natural laws which are the basis of all sciences and arts, so that the child may better understand

and participate in the marvellous things which civilization creates.

Speeding up the march of civilization and at the same time being in touch with Nature create a difficult social problem. It thus becomes a duty of society to satisfy the needs of the child at the various stages of development, if the child and consequently society and mankind are not to go under but are to advance on the road of progress.

The Houses of Children are intended to solve the above social problems. They are a result of civilization and they are intended to solve the problems created by civilization.

In the case of the walk we have described, the adult follows the child and sees what are the things which interests the child and allows him to follow his natural needs; so in the Houses of Children we follow the child and allow him to go forward; and from his revelation we discover his needs and assist him to satisfy those needs.

16

SCIENCE

OF CHILDHOOD

The science of childhood is now better studied and understood than in previous times.

It was only towards the middle of the last century that this science was seriously thought about. Up to the beginning of this century studies of childhood were mostly mere observations which did not require much scientific acumen.

At the beginning of this century the results of child study were the following: it was observed that the child likes to play; that the child likes to imitate; and that the child likes to hear stories. Action was taken on the above observations in an organized fashion in certain institutions and in a loose manner in the homes.

As scientific interest in childhood increased the language of the child was studied. What the child said and the words he used were carefully taken down and these records ran into volumes. Though the interest shown in the study of childhood was an honour to the child, the study itself was rather superficial. Yet these early researches were significant because they laid the foundation for child psychology.

Then a fortunate thing happened to focus the mind of thinkers on the science of childhood. Professor William James, a great and much-loved leader in the field of psychology, compared the child to a butterfly which goes from flower to flower but gathers very little nectar. He said that the child had no ability to fix his attention. He added that "the whole possibility of education depends on the child; and if anyone could fix the child's attention then all the problems of education could be solved".

When an authority like William James made a statement like the one above, all the minor stars endorsed his opinion and repeated what was untrue: that the child's mind was unstable and the child was unable to fix his attention long enough on anything so as to understand it; that it was objects that attracted the mind of the child; and that the child's mind was unable to fix attention on objects. This was all wrong.

But on account of the popularity and great influence of William James his statement brought the child into the limelight. The observation, though incorrect, focussed the attention of the world on the child. It was as if a great monarch had passed through a crowd and stopped to pay attention to a definite person and thereby the attention of the whole crowd was drawn to that person.

No one had paid much attention to the science of childhood before. Now several thinkers became interested.

Thus during the first years of this century psychologists began to study the child systematically. Scientific methods were applied to the study of childhood.

Mental tests carefully devised were adopted; the things which the child said and did were observed and recorded.

In this manner taking into account the cursory observations of previous ages, psychologists concentrated on the three aspects of a child's behaviour already mentioned, namely how the child grew in imitation; how the child grew in play; and how the child grew in imagination. It must be noted that the above researches were concerned not with the inner pattern or powers of the mind but with the external activities concerned in the development of the child. This was the first notable epoch in the progress of the science of childhood.

The second epoch which followed was full of enthusiasm for the unexpected performances of small children.

There was a realization that the method of functioning of a child's mind was different from the method of functioning of an adult's mind; and that, mentally, small children are able to do things far above their expected capacity.

We shall give an example: A mother in order to have a peaceful preparation for Christmas sent her child of three and a half to a Kindergarten for three weeks. Each of the seven children in the class had to learn to recite a small Christmas poem or carol. Two surprising things followed. The first surprising thing was that each child had learnt in such a short time the poem taught to him. The second surprising thing was that each child had learnt each of the six poems intended to be learnt by the remaining children. Further all the children had mastered the gestures and the details of tone and action which should accompany the recitation of the seven poems.

How did the child of three and a half years manage to do what his elder brother was unable to do? Here was an indication that a small child under certain circumstances was capable of better performance in certain things than older children.

Here is another example. A mother had a book of pictures with a caption written under each picture. The mother read these captions on four evenings to the child while the child was looking at the pictures. This was a small child who had not learnt to read anything. Yet on the fifth evening the mother found that the child was able to repeat the names of the pictures in the exact sequence without looking at the pictures, though there was no connection between the different pictures in the book.

This point was carefully studied and it was found that the child of three and a half years could easily learn lines of verse without any continuity of thought or meaning and that the older child not only found it more difficult to learn such lines of verse but needed a logical connection of ideas between the lines to help him to learn them. Even in the latter case the younger children were able to learn the lines more easily.

It must be remembered that the small children cannot read and therefore had to depend only on spoken words to help their memory. On the other hand, the older children had the advantage of being able to read. Yet their performance in remembering was not so good as that of the younger children. Psychologists explain this phenomenon by saying that the very fact of reading the lines caused an interruption in the mind of the older child and obstructed memorization. The fact is that psychologists at this stage did not believe that younger children could do certain things more easily than older ones.

The investigation showed another characteristic of the mind of the child of three and a half years of age. In relation to younger children it has been pointed out that their mind was like the sensitive film of the camera. But children of three and a half years of age reveal a remarkable clearness and precision in the reception and retention of impressions as if words and facts were engraved on some stone tablets in their minds.

As an example we may mention the experiments of a psychologist with stories related to children of three and a half years. This psychologist related a story to a child of this age once; then when relating the story a second time he varied the story, the child said: "No, No, it is not like that." When in the second recital a fact was omitted or a name changed, the child promptly made the necessary correction. The above accuracy of reception and retention has been observed in the generality of children of this age.

The same thing has been observed in relation to mastery of verses without any sequence of ideas. It is this firmness of impression which we have explained by saying figuratively that the data presented to the child are being as it were sculptured in the mind. If such is the performance of the child of this age in relation to abstract symbols of language, we may infer his facility in the absorption of more perceptible and verifiable objects.

A third stage in the science of childhood was developed when the Houses of Children were established. We grasped a law of nature by which children have certain definite periods of sensitivity when there is a facility for the absorption of certain aspects of the environment: one of these periods is the period of sensitivity for language and words of all kinds.

It was Mario Montessori who was responsible for the suggestion that at this period of sensitivity when children have a voracious appetite for words, it would be more useful to allow them to master words relating to reality than words relating to things of fantasy. Thus the children were given facilities for acquiring scientific terms in direct association with the objects they denoted. As mentioned in a previous chapter children were allowed to acquire in the above manner geometrical terms or geographical or botanical or biological terms. Our experiments showed that in the mastery of scientific terms children of three and a half years did better than children of five years.

It is true that earlier psychologists and educators gave words to the children; but they made the children learn poems of fancy and fairy tales, and plenty of them. Our procedure was to allow children to master spontaneously words in association with objects of reality so that later acquisition of scientific knowledge might be facilitated.

One important contribution Dr. Montessori has made to the science of childhood is the discovery and demonstration of successive periods of sensitivity in which the child performs certain functions and makes certain acquisitions more easily and more spontaneously than in earlier or later periods. The methods and materials of education in our Houses of Children have been based on the ascertained secrets of childhood.

Another secret of childhood on which much interest has been centred is play. It is clear that play has an important bearing on the development of the child. It is also clear that the characteristics of play are: the activity of the child at play is not ordered or commanded by an adult and the aim of the play or the activity involved in it is the play or the activity itself and nothing beyond. Another characteristic is that after choosing some activity in the form of play the child repeats it over and over again.

The characteristic in play which has been exalted by some writers is the doing of a thing for the sake of doing it. What we as educators have to emphasize is nature's plan in implanting the love of play in the child to aid the child's development. We have to note the incipient idealism in doing work for work's sake, the perseverance in carrying it out and the frequent repetition of an activity for the sake of obtaining facility in the work itself.

Before our Houses of Children were established it was usual to direct the child's natural impulse to play with toys and playthings. If the child is confined to toys and playthings there is no doubt that its activities of play will be round toys and playthings and nothing more. This practice is similar to the old method of giving children fanciful poems and fairy tales during the sensitive period of their lives when they were hungry for words and real knowledge.

In our Houses of Children we respond to the child's natural love of play but we bring the play activities of the child close to reality. One has to study the materials and apparatus in our Houses of Children and the performance of exercises of practical life and sensorial exercises there by the children to realize how beneficially the play activities of the children can be offered to present facts instead of fancies and reality instead of fiction. It is clearly seen that the pleasure of play activity is increased by this contact with reality.

It may be said that the sensorial exercises which may be seen in our Houses of Children have their obvious value but the exercises of practical life are mere imitations of adult life. It must be remembered that most of the activities of the child including play activity are inspired by observation. The exercises of practical life are formative activities. They involve inspiration, repetition and concentration on precise details. They take into account the natural impulses of the special periods of childhood. Though for the moment the exercises have no merely practical aims, they are a work of adaptation to the environment. Such adaptation to the environment and efficient functioning therein is the very essence of a useful education.

17

WRITTEN LANGUAGE AND HUMAN PROGRESS

Mankind is visibly evolving. There are many aspects of this evolution; many groups of people undergoing this process in a particular way. The link that connects one generation with another to form a chain of evolution is the child.

The discovery of sounds and words to express thoughts is one of the greatest of human discoveries. For a long time all thoughts and all knowledge were transmitted from generation to generation by the spoken word. The increasing burden of knowledge became so heavy that the human mind could not support it. Then occurred an event of momentous importance in human progress. This is the invention of written language. Written language helped individuals and nations to preserve what memory could no longer retain. It may be stated that no event in history had such far-reaching effects as the advent of written language.

The evolution of spoken language itself was a marvel. The invention of written language was a much greater marvel. It is one of the first instances of man's achievement that goes beyond the powers and possibilities of nature. With the invention of written language man put himself above nature and started a long and glorious campaign of conquests over nature. It is a triumph that is entirely due to man's own efforts.

Written language has a history of thousands of years behind it. A supranatural impulse at a decisive point of time brought about the creation of the alphabet. With the creation of the alphabet, written language or the writing of thoughts in words made an enormous advance. An important aspect of the invention of written language was its use in the writing of history and the continued record of world events.

WRITTEN LANGUAGE AND HUMAN PROGRESS

One must realize that an alphabet is not merely a particular series of signs and letters; for there are so many alphabets and so many languages. The essence of the invention of the alphabet was the fundamental idea behind it. That idea was that by means of signs representing individual sounds of the spoken language (letters) human thoughts could be preserved and transmitted from individual to individual and from generation to generation. This grand concept has led to the existence of so many alphabets the development of which has been an invaluable contribution to the advancement of the human race.

There was a time when ideas were expressed by means of pictures. This was a poor medium. There was rigidity about it and it was unserviceable for the expression of abstract ideas or principles. If that system had continued it would have been impossible for mankind to have made the progress which has been made.

Written language is something different from spoken language, though the former is an invention based on the latter. It was difficult enough for nations and communities to evolve, through long periods of time, sufficient and suitable words to describe the objects around them, to express the thoughts of the mind, and the emotions of the heart. The invention and elaboration of written language have made it possible for man to transmit and to convey not only ideas and emotions but also to formulate or explain principles and laws and every item of impression formed in the mind.

Incidentally one is obliged to observe that the capacity of language to absorb every bit of knowledge or experience is similar to the capacity of a young child to absorb and register, during certain periods of sensitivity, items of knowledge and experience from his environment.

The implements and materials used in writing have their own history of progress. The surfaces used for writing at the early stages were those of stones, skins, barks and tissues of trees; the writing instruments used were of iron, wood and paint-brush.

At first there were a few men, great in their generation, who could convey their thoughts in written language. They were priests, philosophers or poets who were regarded as men of culture. Their influence was remarkable. While written language was being prepared and perfected, the majority of children were growing in a simple and unlettered environment.

Then came another stage when people who had abandoned their pastoral or agricultural life for commercial enterprises, found in written language a useful ally to send commercial communications to distant places. The merchant princes wanted written languages, code words and figures. Written language caught up by the currents of commerce spread out among the powerful people of the earth. The simple and humble people all over the world had no chance of handling this weapon. Some of them expressed their aspiration by saying: "How nice it would be if I knew how to write!" They had to go to a specialist called a public writer to get a letter written; they had to go to a literate person in the village to get a letter read.

The inability to write began to be felt as an inferiority and as an obstacle. The inadequacy of the possession of only spoken language was felt more and more intensely until 150 years ago when people rose and rebelled against many civil disabilities; and in their declaration of the rights of man they included the right of each individual to obtain facilities to master and use the great instrument of written language. Thus it became a matter of universal demand that man could not live in the midst of modern civilization without the ability to write letters and figures. It was insisted that written language, which was the acquisition of some, must become the possession of all. The right for facilities to learn written language was one of the rights of democracy, established by bloodshed and revolution by countries which have been the greatest champions of human freedom. This democratic spirit has permeated a large part of the globe. In many countries universal and compulsory education has been inaugurated as a foundation for national advancement.

Voluntary education existed earlier but compulsory education marks a new epoch in history. Nations have broken a barricade in front of them and have gone forward. It has been recognized as a fundamental right of every citizen to be able to read, to write and to reckon (the three 'R's). In the meantime the rapidity of production and increase in the quality of writing paper, the perfection reached in the varieties of pens and writing implements, the invention of printing and the unprecedented developments in printing methods and printing machinery have given written language indescribable power and potency in human affairs.

With national plans for the universalization of literacy, and the tremendous facilities for the purpose supplied by science and discovery and the manufacturing industries, the stage is set for an unparalleled intensification of human thought and activity. But there is something strange about the behaviour of the adult. After winning the right to aquire such an instrument of progress as literacy, the parents do not take the trouble to acquire literacy themselves but in almost all countries the task was imposed upon the children. Here is an apparent inconsistency which needs consideration.

Why should parents who are the natural defenders of their children place on children burdens which they themselves think irksome? The reason is that there are forces impinging upon the evolution of humanity which sometimes overpower even those instincts given by nature for the care of the species. Thus society feels an impulse to undertake activity to adapt itself to new conditions and circumstances. The adult being less adaptable and the child being more adaptable to new conditions and circumstances, society imposes on the child burdens necessary for the onward march of mankind. The task of education is then accompanied by an effort to lighten the burden of the child and to allow him to find happiness in his active adaptation to his changing environment.

18

ONE PLAN AND MANY

Cosmic
Plan.

PATTERNS

There is a plan to which the whole universe is subject. All things, animate and inanimate, are subordinated to that plan. There are also patterns for each species of living and non-living things. These patterns fall in line with the universal plan.

Everything in Nature, according to its own laws of development, approximates to the pattern of perfection applicable to itself. There is an urge in every individual of every species to fit into the appropriate pattern. There is also an inevitableness with which all patterns fit into the great plan.

From the seed to the full grown tree, from the egg to the adult hen, from the embryo to the man of maturity, the striving to embody a pattern is perceptible. It takes a loftier vision to understand and appreciate how all creatures and all things evolve into infinite varieties of patterns with a magnificent impulse to subordinate themselves to the central plan of the universe.

It is certain that the urge to protect the offspring and to conserve the species is among the strongest of all urges of nature. But there is a purpose higher than the protection of the offspring or the preservation of the species. This purpose is something beyond mere growing according to a pattern or living according to instincts. This higher purpose is to conform to a master plan towards which all things are moving.

The imposition of a hard task like compulsory education on the child, even to enable him to read, write and reckon, appears at first sight to be against nature. But it is clear that society has the intuition to feel that children can perform the task of adaptation to new conditions and circumstances better than adults and that the adaptation is necessary for the edification and evolution of mankind. This task imposed on the child need not have become a tyranny and an infliction as it did. To demonstrate that over and above adhering to a pattern of existence there is conformity to a higher plan, we shall give some examples from Nature.

The cow is one of the most important land animals. Its purpose is not merely to look after itself and its calf. Apart from self-preservation and the preservation of the species, its one duty in the cosmic plan is the maintenance of grass lands and meadows in good condition. The cow is one of the greatest sustainers of agriculture. Zoologically the cow was one of the latest animals to appear on the face of the earth. Its advent synchronized with the appearance of large tracts of grass lands in various parts of the earth. It is a matter of scientific knowledge that to keep grass lands in good condition the grass must be kept cut short to the ground; that the ground should be pressed down to assist growth; and that the ground should be fertilized. The cow does all these things besides looking after itself and its progeny.

The obedience of the cow to this great cosmic mandate is wonderful. For ages and centuries the cow has done this service. The old theory of evolution that the personal needs of the animal evolved specialized organs does not meet the case: for, the cow was strong enough to have found other means of satisfying its needs with less trouble. But it stuck to its cosmic task: it continued eating grass although grass is so indigestible and the cellulose in it is so difficult to break up that it involves four stomachs to deal with the problem of digestion. The cow could have found more easily digestible food, but readily enough it follows the cosmic plan.

If one studies the matter carefully, one sees that every animal and everything in Nature, in addition to following a pattern of its own existence, has a special task for the common welfare of the cosmos. In the seas certain animals keep the quantity of salt in sea water in correct proportion by efforts which are not so much beneficial to themselves as to others. If the salt in the waters of the sea were not kept in correct proportion there would be an end to the life of the multitudes of living beings in the seas and consequently life on the land surface would be equally affected. How do these special marine animals perform their important cosmic task? It has been found that they drink many times their own weight of water fixing the salts in it so as to keep down the proportion of salt in the sea water.

Equally significant is the cosmic work of other living beings which consume and diminish poisonous gases in the atmosphere. The poisonous gases which for ages have been thrown into the air as the result of cosmic eruptions could have put an end to life on earth but the danger has been avoided by the cosmic work of plants and trees which consume these gases and reduce their quantity below the danger level. While they serve the so-called selfish purpose of preserving themselves and their species, plants and trees are conforming to the requirements of an all-embracing plan.

We may also mention the cosmic task of those birds which eat carrion and corpses in putrefaction. They can easily eat living animals but they remain faithful to their function of cleaning the earth of things dangerous to other beings.

So in every cosmic detail, from the maintenance of the purity of air to the maintenance of the purity of water, each living thing performs its task with fidelity to a definite plan. So does all creation. The suns and the stars in their movements; the earth and the planets in their rotations and revolutions; the clouds condensing into showers; plants and animals in their cycles of birth, growth and decay; the oceans and rivers, minerals and metals and all kinds of matter in their formations and functions; from the earthworm that burrows into the earth to the butterfly that flies round and round and perches on the flowers; all things in Nature have a pattern to which they conform and all of them adhere to a plan into which they weave themselves to form a universe in equilibrium. They function for the preservation of the whole according to a plan and for the preservation of the species according to a pattern; thus are brought about order and harmony in Nature.

The discovery of written language had a far reaching effect on the pattern of life. Man, who was accustomed to talk only with his tongue, was able to hear with his eyes and speak with his hands. Here was a method not only of garnering and propagating knowledge and experience and enlarging the patterns of life but also of aiding the momentum of cosmic evolution.

Compulsory education imposed a heavy duty on children. This duty was partly in the interests of children. But the children were also rendering a service to the world in helping the progress of civilization.

It was as if a new conquest had to be made by man. A call came to the children like the call of Alexander the Great: "Follow me to the conquest of the world." All children of ages suitable for this warfare were mobilized. They had to march forward with suffering and pain. Children under five years were excluded from the forces; those of six years and over were conscripted for service and they were regimented and drilled in certain school subjects. But this service has been a martyrdom of the child.

19

THE MARTYRDOM OF

THE CHILD

Compulsory education had the best intentions behind it. The progress of the individual, of the nation, and of mankind was aimed at. The urge for this forward leap of mankind was irresistible. But adults having secured the rights of education put the whole burden on the child.

For a long, long time education has been a martyrdom for the child. Much health and happiness of the child were sacrificed for the sake of education. It is not necessary to be a Doctor of Medicine or a mental expert to describe the physical and mental illness directly produced by education in the past.

Many books have been written not on the illnesses of childhood but on the illnesses caused by the schools themselves. When one reads them one will see records of the organs and functions of the child damaged by schools.

Skeletons, muscles, and nerves were adversely affected. Digestion and mental faculties were seriously interfered with. In several cases pathological conditions of both body and mind were brought about by schooling and the schools.

To deal with the trouble a simple method was devised. The Governments in different countries laid down rules of hygiene and enforced them in the schools. The attempt was to cure the illnesses of the schools. There was no attempt to remove the causes of the illnesses. The curative method did not eradicate the maladies.

Towards the end of the last century the conditions became worse. Volumes were written to show that schools had failed to develop character, intelligence or moral behaviour; that pupils had contracted habits of lying, deceit or laziness; that they were incapable of concentrating attention or thinking adequately on a subject; and that the schools were responsible for creating in pupils a hatred towards the teacher and an aversion to learning.

The attitude of the pupil was: "Thank God, the teacher is ill," or "How can we hoodwink the teacher and get out of the class room?" The children were so incapable of observation that they could not observe any danger on the roads. They came yelling out of the schools, knocking one another down, hurling books at one another, running in the middle of the streets, oblivious of the inconvenience to passengers or the danger from moving vehicles to themselves. Significantly in front of many schools facing roads a notice was put up as follows: "School: Take care."

There was again a period of caution in many ways. Care was taken so that children might not be run over by cars or vehicles. Care was taken not to allow them to injure their sight, not to get hunch-backed by bad posture in the schools and not to injure each other. It was all negative action. The root causes were left in the system itself.

Then a doubt arose as to whether so much education was necessary. Some people thought that difficulties could be reduced by reducing the quantity and quality of education. They said there was too much mental exhaustion caused to the children. Their aim was: What could be taken out of the syllabus?

They looked at the matter from the adult's point of view. They argued: "We don't see any use of geometry in adult life; omit geometry from the syllabus." Of arithmetic their opinion was: "Just enough to enable children to buy and sell things; the rest may be omitted." They asserted: "What is the use of grammar, so long as children can speak and write without it? We can drop it from the syllabus."

Little by little school work was reduced till children were doing next to nothing regarding mental work. In fact people were convinced that it was too early to send children of six years of age to school: that they would be able to learn everything necessary if they went to school at eight years of age.

Little study, much play, and more games became the fashion. Punishment was reluctantly retained to placate teachers. Examinations too would have disappeared but the question was raised "How can we know what the child knows if there are no examinations?" So, school-leaving examinations were maintained.

WHAT YOU SHOULD KNOW ABOUT YOUR CHILD

When compulsory instruction was getting lighter, sports and games were made compulsory. In fact in some schools children who were good at boxing or football were allowed to pass easy examinations in school subjects. The examinations which the others had to take up were not so easy.

The shortening of school hours and the simplification of syllabuses did not improve education. The result was the production of men and women wanting in knowledge, wanting in discipline and wanting in character.

Then there was a revolt against the softening of children's bodies and minds. People said, let us go back to the point from which we started. This culminated, under Mussolini, Hitler and Tojo, in mental and moral atrophy and concentration on physical regimentation and military efficiency.

This is the state of confusion out of which an education for the future had to arise.

If education is to be an aid to civilization, it cannot be carried out by emptying the schools of knowledge, of character, of discipline, of social harmony, and above all, of freedom. Education has thus become a momentous problem.

The main problem is the problem of freedom: its significance and repercussions have to be clearly understood. The adult's idea that freedom consists in minimizing duties and obligations must be rejected. We must also reject the idea that the joy of a child is in being forced to play all the time or the major part of the day.

The foundation of education must be based on the following facts: that the joy of the child is in accomplishing things well for his age; that the real satisfaction of the child is to give maximum effort to the task in hand; that happiness consists in well-directed activity of body and mind in the way of excellence; that strength of mind and body and spirit is acquired by exercise and experience; and that true freedom has, as its objective, service to society and to mankind consistent with the progress and happiness of the individual.

The freedom that is given to the child is not liberation from parents and teachers; it is not freedom from the laws of Nature or of the state or of society, but the utmost freedom for self-development and self-realization compatible with service to society.

THE MARTYRDOM OF THE CHILD

When one sees trees, plants and flowers in a garden or fishes in the sea one gets an impression of the freedom of life. Supposing our idea of freedom was freedom not to obey any laws we should logically say: "Those poor plants are tied to their roots; let us pull them out and make them free," or "It is a pity that the fishes are condemned to stay in the water the whole time; let us make them free by taking them out."

We have to observe that by the very act of giving freedom as above we are taking away life itself. In several respects the same remark applies to the child. Are we going to free the child from work? Such attempts will be like uprooting a plant or taking a fish out of water.

When we understand the basic reality we find that the freedom of the child is in the joy of search, of knowledge, of action, and of service. As the muscle becomes strong with exercise, so do joy and strength grow with activity, exertion, and achievement.

Yet the martyrdom of the child for the advancement of society was real. If you summon a meeting of adults to propagate some new or potent ideas, how few of them attend the meeting? Even those who do attend, hear you for an hour and disappear. But in the case of children they are kept together for days, months, and years under the control and direction of their educators. He who wishes to influence mankind knows that he can do this by gathering children together and keeping them at school. This advantage, despite its abuse and despite the maltreatment of the child through ignorance or indifference, has been responsible in the main for a forward step in civilization.

With the beginning of this century there was an awakening of the adult to the dangers and evils which school life brought upon children. Attention was directed to the fact that when the child suffers he cannot rebel or defend himself. Society which submits the child to education must undertake the responsibility of defending the child. The adult who was the oppressor of the child must become its liberator. The conscience of the adult must be awakened if the freedom of the child is to be a reality. The only reaction of the child to bad treatment is greater weakness and diminished mental and physical powers.

From this point of view education remains an all-pervading social question. Freedom for the child within the laws of its own development is freedom for society and mankind. Though the martyrdom of the child since the beginning of compulsory education produced some beneficial results, yet if the conscience of society is aroused and the scientific knowledge of childhood is harnessed to service, better results are bound to follow; for given the proper conditions, the exercise of human faculties of body, mind and spirit are ordained to give pleasure, not pain.

20

WORK AND DISCIPLINE

The secret of a happy life is congenial work. Work is purposeful activity. Man is the foremost worker in creation. Man's work has changed the face of the earth.

The emphasis on freedom is for the development of individuality. The emphasis on discipline is for the benefit of the individual and of society. Just as work and rest can go together, so it is possible to reconcile freedom and discipline, the individual and society. The contrasts are more accentuated by the progress of civilization.

Civilization demands more work. Social life demands more discipline. Society decreases the bounds of individual freedom. There can be no progress without work. Freedom is necessary. So is discipline. Both are wanted for the advancement of the individual and society.

Yet workers of all kinds want less work, more renumeration, more leisure, more amusement and better conditions of life. Workers of the same category have formed unions and make their demands against their employers. The contest between labour and capital is an increasing problem.

At the beginning of this century the same tendency was reflected from the society of adults to the society of children at school. The result was fewer days at school, fewer hours of work, shorter lessons, increased sports and more games. The object was to protect children against fatigue and give them more rest.

In this connection a curious fact was observed. Although less work and more recreation were the order of the day, the health of the children was no better. And there was evidence of greater fatigue than before. It was also found that after working continuously for a comparatively long period like 90 minutes on a subject, children showed less signs of mental fatigue and more restfulness than when they worked for 45 minutes only.

The reason is this. The mind takes some time to develop interest, to be set in motion, to get warmed up into a subject, to attain a state of profitable work. If at this time there is interruption, not only is a period of profitable work lost, but the interruption produces an unpleasant sensation which is identical with fatigue.

Fatigue is also caused by work unsuitable to the individual. Suitable work reduces fatigue on account of the pleasure derived from the work itself. Thus the two causes of fatigue are unsuitable work and premature interruption of work.

If we turn to the Houses of Children we observe something strange. Left to themselves the children work ceaselessly; they do not worry about the clock. Another strange thing is that after long and continuous activity the childrens' capacity for work does not appear to diminish but to improve.

In fact a topsy-turvy situation arises. The children find joy, satisfaction and exhilaration in work. More work seems to produce more restfulness. After much energy has been spent in doing work, the very expenditure seems to produce a still larger quantity of energy.

In order to produce a satisfactory output of work, there must be not only suitable occupation but also suitable conditions. Among these are proper food, fresh air, and sunlight. The Houses of Children and the materials and environment provided there are an illustration of occupation and conditions suitable to the age and capacity of the workers.

When proper conditions are given and body and mind are exercised the child grows joyously and harmoniously. The more exercise there is, the more fresh the child's life becomes. Work thus becomes the *sine-qua-non* of growth, development, efficiency and happiness.

The questions of freedom and discipline are connected with work. Given the necessary freedom, suitable materials and environment, what the child longs for is work. When the environment, as in the Houses of Children, induces and prompts the required activity, the problem of discipline solves itself.

The essence of good discipline may be illustrated by a remark from a leading Japanese educationist who visited a Montessori demonstration class in San Francisco and who, after watching the children at work, said: "I like everything in your school except the exaggerated discipline!" Now, this discipline was the result of freedom. Discipline and freedom are so co-related that, if there is some lack of discipline, the cause is to be found in some lack of freedom.

In the same way if there is some disorder in our Houses of Children we presume some imposition from outside. When there is disorder or lack of discipline, under the conditions in our Houses of Children, the fault is with the adult, not with the children. The directress has misunderstood something and in some way has attempted to enslave the children. The consequence is disorder or want of discipline. This is no doubt natural discipline in a special environment.

Can this be copied by society which has obviously to abide by some rules? The matter has been carefully studied. It has been found that children can and will obey orders from without. Nature has implanted in the child an urge to obey. For the right ordering of society we have to build on this urge to obey, though mere mechanical obedience does not result in proper discipline. True obedience must elevate a child and not enslave him.

The urge of obedience is in the child. In some cases there is no account of sheer impossibility. In other cases the child does not know how to obey. He must therefore be given opportunities for exercise in obedience so as to enable him to obey. Discipline would be impossible if not for the urge of obedience in the child. Society would be impossible without readiness to obey laws which hold society together.

Just as a person with a natural talent for music has to be taught to play on a musical instrument and after learning how to play on the instrument, his performances give him repeated pleasure, so if the child grows in obedience, every act of obedience will give him pleasure. The responsibility of those who give orders is always heavy.

The love of activity, the yearning for freedom, the urge for obedience, the impulse to conform to laws which are at the heart of all creation—these qualities make man the unparalleled work of Nature.

Thus the earliest traces of man's life on earth are not his homes or houses, bones or remains, but the implements of his work. It may be said that man in his capacity as worker is responsible for all that is meant by evolution, progress or civilization.

We have seen in our Houses of Children something similar to the endless activity in nature. We don't see in the children any reflection of the reluctance of adults to work. The contrast compels thought. Imagine all classes of workmen asking for more work and still more work; and after having finished the given work, instead of saying that they are tired, asserting "How nice it is to have some more work to do!" Would not such a state be the beginning of a new society in which every person wants to work, and is given congenial work and the proper conditions, and the more he works the more happy he feels?

Does Nature make a difference between work and play or occupation and rest? Watch the unending activity of the flowing stream or the growing tree. See the breakers of the ocean, the unceasing movements of the earth, the planets, the sun and the stars. All creation is life, movement, work. What about our hearts, our lungs, our bloodstream which work continuously from birth till death? Have they asked for some rest? Not even during sleep are they inactive. What about our mind which works without intermission while we are awake or asleep?

21

MONTESSORI HOUSES

OF CHILDREN

The environments and the contents of the Houses of Children, sometimes called Montessori Schools, have been so prepared as to embody the principles stated in the previous chapters. The buildings, furniture, apparatus and other requisites are designed to suit the age and size of the children concerned. The institution provides for self-activity and spontaneous development of children.

There is freedom in the environment. There is discipline which arises out of the environment. There is joy which is the sign of all healthy growth. The conditions provide for mutual understanding, co-operation and helpfulness which are the roots of morality and character.

It is only by a personal visit to a Montessori House of Children and direct inspection that one can understand the aims underlying the activities there. Knowledge of the requirements of childhood is the basis on which the apparatus and the educational materials have been elaborated. This volume is not a book of method. It is concerned with principles.

Dealing with principles it is necessary to indicate the reason for the main activities for which provision is made in Montessori Houses of Children. Besides facilities for health and hygiene and direct contact with natural objects, the activities of children in the early stages are classified as Sensorial Exercises and Exercises of Practical Life.

It may be useful to point out the scientific foundation for the Sensorial Exercises and the Exercises of Practical Life in Montessori Houses of Children.

"There is nothing in the intellect which was not first in the senses" said one of the greatest of thinkers. All elements of our knowledge of the external world are derived through our senses. The five senses are the five gates through which knowledge flows into the mind from birth till death. The mind stores up and elaborates the impressions received through the senses; and by various processes builds up the structure of knowledge.

To understand the fundamental importance of the senses let us consider a person who is born blind. To such a person complete knowledge of the visible world is impossible. He cannot see form or colour. All the visible beauty of the blue hills, all the thrill of setting suns and flowering plants and all the rapture caused by the contemplation of masterpieces of sculpture or painting are to him as good as if they did not exist.

Being unable to see anything, he cannot remember anything that is only visible. Having had no perception of visible things, he has no visual memory of such things. Nor can he imagine anything visible nor think nor reason about only visible aspects with any approximation to reality.

The case of a person born deaf is similar. His mind is a perfect blank as regards all audible things. The charm of music, the sweetness of a friendly voice, and the whole world of sound are shut out from his mind. He cannot perceive any sound nor remember, imagine nor reason about any audible thing whatsoever.

It is difficult to think of a person totally devoid of touch or movement, taste or smell. But any defect in any of the senses means a corresponding incapacity to acquire knowledge or form complete concepts of reality.

An ordinary degree of sharpness of the eyes enables a person to obtain ordinarily accurate impressions from the visible world. The same degree of sharpness of the ears in a similar manner enables a person to gather normal impressions from the world of sound.

It is so with other senses. A person with a defective sense of smell has an inability to apply his mind to the outside world in proportion to the defect of his olfactory sensations. A defect in the sense of taste or touch will adversely affect the mind likewise.

The adverse effect of any defect in the senses is far-reaching. It affects every process or faculty of the mind. A defective sensation of the eye or of the ear or of any other sense produces

defective percepts. The memory therefore holds defective per- *imagi-*
cepts and notions. Imagination will be equally affected, for *nation*
imagination is a reconstruction of perceived images stored up in
the mind. Given that reasoning is inference from data supplied
to the mind, defective data must produce defective reasoning.
Thus all the processes of the mind become tainted with the
defect in any of the senses, in proportion to the degree of defect
in the sense or senses concerned. The tremendous importance of
the senses in the acquisition of knowledge thus becomes clear.

But watch the juggler at the circus keeping six or seven balls
in the air without allowing any of them to drop to the ground by
dexterously catching and throwing up successive balls in
rotation. The performance of the juggler is due to persistent,
continued and skilful training. It involves training of the hand,
of the eye, of muscles, of judgement, of foresight, and of
equilibrium.

In the same way, the performance of the rope-walker, tea-
taster and persons who identify hundreds of drugs by their smell
are due to training.

In other walks of life too we see the value of a proper training
of the senses. To be a good painter, besides the mastery of
technique, a person must have a training in observation and
appreciation of colour and shade, perspective and form. The
telephone operator or stenographer cannot function efficiently
unless the sense of hearing is sound and properly trained. It will
be noticed that the skill of most artisans and craftsmen like
carpenters, masons, blacksmiths, brick-makers, potters and
gem cutters mostly consist in the co-ordinated training of hand
and eye. A successful dancer, a famous musician, the winner of a
blue ribbon in tennis or cricket knows how much of his
excellence was due to persistent and prolonged training.

The effect of training is the same in all activities whether of
the body or the mind. In any work or profession or trade the
mind and body are involved. Certain aspects of the mind, certain
limbs of the body, and one or more of the senses get special
application in various forms of co-ordination and combination.
In the work of a carpenter, it is not merely the hand and
eye that are being exercised. In the game of football it is
not merely the legs and eyes that are used. Clearly, certain
limbs and senses play a prominent part. But the whole body

and mind are generally concerned in the activity and its efficiency.

How is it that many people, both young and old, fail to see or hear or perceive what a trained observer so easily recognizes and identifies? The complaint is ever old and ever new that people having eyes see not and having ears hear not. At the bottom of all defective knowledge are non-observation and mal-observation; or the failure to observe things and inaccurate observation of things. Hence the necessity to prepare, as in Montessori Houses of Children, an environment which will direct the mind spontaneously to observe what has to be observed and where conditions will prevent errors of observation. The value of training is as important in the constructive arts and the practical occupations of life as in scientific method.

It is for these reasons that the group of exercises organized in Montessori Houses of Children called Sensorial Exercises go hand in hand with the group of exercises called Exercises of Practical Life. The training thus becomes training for life.

The training in the above exercises is only one aspect of Montessori education in the early stages. The training is carried out comprehensively and directly. The training is on real objects and by means of real objects. The training brings the child face to face with concrete items of reality.

Montessori education, unlike the old education, is not education mainly in words or through words. Montessori education is education mainly in things and through things. This attitude has been elucidated in previous chapters. The significance of language has been dealt with.

The items of material objects and apparatus have been devised, collected, graded and placed in the room or in the environment of the child for a set purpose and according to a purposeful design. The plan, structure and contents of a good Montessori House of Children are based on a knowledge of the developmental requirements of various stages of child-hood.

The old education laid emphasis on teaching by the teacher and learning by the learner. The Montessori Method lays emphasis on observation and discovery by the child. It lays emphasis on the provision of facilities and protection for the child by the directress.

MONTESSORI HOUSES OF CHILDREN

The Montessori Method itself has been developed by means of observation and discovery. The principles stated in these chapters were not first enumerated and then applied to education so as to evolve the Montessori Method. The Montessori Method was first evolved by experiment and experience and by the process of observation and discovery. Benefit to the child and the needs of Society were the criteria. The principles are aids to test the method. The best proof is its success in the development of the child, in the child's love of achievement and service to society.

Fundamentally, Montessori education energizes and vivifies those aids to noble life which are within. Hence, the insistence on principles which have been emphasized in this book.